"Unlike a lot of writers, Maxey does not embellish the Second World War. He lets it speak for itself as he helps to push the conflict across Europe after D-Day. Uncertainty . . . boredom . . . uncertaintly . . . terror. That's the pattern—and always with the big question hanging over each day: 'Will I live or will I die?' Maxey has, in other words, sent a telegram from inside what George Marshall called 'the fog of war.' "

—Harry Miles Muheim, Lt., USNR (Ret.)

"Bill Maxey informs the reader in plain but moving language what it took in character, commitment, and plain guts to move a mighty Allied Army of British, French, Canadian, and American soldiers from Normandy to Germany and end Nazi tyranny. The world owes a debt to him and the thousands that participated in this historic undertaking that saved civilization, a debt that never can be repaid."

—Frank A. Bauman

"As another lieutenant in this area, at that time of combat, it is refreshing to read an account of World War II that is as authentic as Major Maxey's coverage of the VII Corps' part in the great fracas. Maxey is a combat soldier who tells it like it was."

—Lt. Col. Russell L. Kelch, USA Ret.

"Three cheers to the author of *Come with Me to a War*! He has written an excellent war story. This book should be read over and over again. It is exciting and moves at a fast pace."

—Leland T. Watson, Jr.
Dottie Watson
Curators, Great Lakes Naval Museum Association, Inc.

"The cover says it all. *Come with Me to a War*, by William Maxey, is the story of the VII Corps in Europe from D-Day to VE Day, based on his personal experiences as a general's aide. Written by a 'headquarters man,' the book is refreshing in its portrayal of some of the duties, responsibilities, and benefits of being an aide. Those interested in reading straightforward personal accounts of the European campaign will find this book well worth their time."

—John Wiggin
Napa, California

"For authenticity and accuracy, Bill Maxey's first-person account of his experiences in World War II rank with anything written about the Great Conflict—with no exceptions. As a serious churchman, Bill couln't bring himself to quote exactly what Gen. McAuliffe replied when the Germans told him to surrender. But we now know it wasn't 'Nuts!' as history records. It's that kind of attention to detail that sets *Come with Me to a War* apart and makes it must reading for Americans who desire to know what kind of war the U.S. fought in Europe and exactly what our fighting forces endured.

—William H. Schroeder
Chairman/Publisher
Lakeland Publishers Inc.
Grayslake, Ill. 60030

"*Come with Me to a War* is more than an engaging and exciting narrative of one man's war from the beaches of Normandy to Eastern Germany. Bill Maxey's can-do determination, courage, and spirit are the hallmarks of his World War II generation. His story is the on-the-spot raw material of history."

—J. Kenneth Brody
Historian, Author of *The Avoidable War*

"Bill, just finished your wonderful book for the second time. It was better this time because I felt even more involved. It is written the way most World War II books wish they were. It brought home to me what you and your comrades really went through and I felt I was there, seeing it all, and experiencing it all firsthand. I now know what my older brother, who was there also, was trying to tell me."

—Calvin F. Gwynne

COME WITH ME TO A WAR

The Story of VII Corps U.S. Army
in Europe

from
D-Day to VE Day

As experienced and told by
William W. Maxey, Major, C.E., USAR Retired

VANTAGE PRESS
New York

Originally compiled by: Lt. William W. Maxey A.D.C. to Brigadier General Williston B. Palmer, VII Corps Artillery Commander during D-Day invasion and until Sept. '44, when assigned to the G-2 (intelligence) section, until March '45, when promoted to VII Corps Public Relations Officer.

The dust cover for this book is a photocopy of a portion of a damaged camouflage parachute which hung from an apple tree over my foxhole the first night in Normandy (D+3). This was near St. Mère Eglise. The VII on the red star was our shoulder patch.

FIRST EDITION

All rights reserved, including the right of
reproduction in whole or in part in any form

Copyright © 1997 by William W. Maxey, Major, C.E., USAR Retired

Published by Vantage Press, Inc.
516 West 34th Street, New York, New York 10001

Manufactured in the United States of America
ISBN: 0-533-12173-6

Library of Congress Catalog Card No.: 96-90794

0 9 8 7 6 5 4 3 2

Contents

Foreword   vii
Prelude   ix

I.	England	1
II.	Utah Beach and the Capture of Cherbourg	7
III.	The Hedgerow Fighting	38
IV.	The Breakthrough	43
V.	The Great Defensive Battle of Mortain	61
VI.	The Falaise Gap and Rapid Move to the Seine	65
VII.	The South Belgium Campaign	74
VIII.	The Push to the Roer River	115
IX.	The Belgian Bulge	132
X.	The Push to the Rhine	147
XI.	The Final Stage	157

Epilogue   171
The Basics (poem)   176

Foreword

This book is an account of the experiences of a junior officer who was fortunate enough to be plucked from more hazardous duty—a field artillery forward observer—and assigned to duty with a corps headquarters. The fortunes of war are fickle. Sometimes you are tossed into the fire. Other times, by a stroke of luck, you are placed in the enviable position of observing the fire and even occasionally tending that fire.

Using the factual morning report as a trellis, or framework, then, I have woven in my personal experiences and observations as I was carried along in this wild river of events called "a war." For a young, small-town boy, it was enlightening, frightening, entertaining, heartbreaking, and above all, maturing.

So here is an opportunity to share one soldier's thoughts and reactions in a rather unique perspective—sometimes in combat, always close to it.

Photographs are primarily from my own collection of over 300 pictures taken in action. These include slave labor camp, photos of POWs, candid photos of "Ike," "Monty," and others. "Operation Tiger," D-Day photos, and D + 6 pictures are by others.

This augmented rewrite, after a fifty-year interlude, is in response to suggestions and encouragement by a new friend, Frank A. Bauman, and expert editing by Harry Miles Muheim and J. Kenneth Brody. Lt. Col. Russell Kelch provided material and expert comments by phone throughout the many months it took to complete this work.

Based on my photos and description of the events, my good friend of long standing, Trig Watson, a talented artist, created a sketch aerial view of the site of our AA/AT gun capture near Valognes. All this was capped off by the patience of my wife Caroline. To these and numerous others who contributed time and expertise, I will always be indebted. Modest in scale though it is, I found it to be more of a challenge than anticipated, and equally enjoyable.

The adventure discussed here, and indeed my entire military career of over twenty years, emanated from a seed sown by a high school classmate and good friend, then Sgt. Richard R. Bentley, who encouraged me to bring my trumpet and join the 129th Infantry, 33rd Division, Illinois National Guard Band in March of 1938. Thank you, Richard.

—William W. Maxey
Major, C.E., USAR Retired

Prelude

This is England. The date is 28 April 1944. Gen. Dwight D. Eisenhower has been appointed Supreme Allied Commander, European Theater of Operations; Field Marshal Bernard L. Montgomery has been appointed Army Ground Forces Commander; and (pertinent to this document) 47-year-old and youthful-looking Maj. Gen. J. Lawton Collins, USA, has been given command of the U.S. VII Corps with Brig. Gen. Williston B. Palmer, USA, as his VII Corps Artillery Commander.

"Operation Overlord," the invasion of Normandy, has been planned and final preparations are being made. General Collins and his VII Corps, composed of the 4th, 9th, 79th, and 90th Infantry Divisions, as well as the 82nd and 101st Airborne Divisions, supported by the Rangers and numerous other special units, have been assigned Utah Beach on the extreme right flank of the operation.

The infantry has been undergoing intensive field training and inspections; the Airborne are extending their training to include night jumps. It will be the night before D-Day when they go. The Rangers are honing their skills. Morale and determination are at a peak. Staff at all levels are working out solutions based upon the most pessimistic predictions. Wooded areas and byways are lined with camouflaged supplies, as well as tanks, trucks, half-tracks, artillery, bridge-building equipment, and road-building equipment.

Overhead—near coastal areas, large cities, and other vital areas—barrage balloons float, tethered by cables designed to snag the unwary German bomber or fighter pilot. Ike has commented, after inspecting all the supplies and equipment, that if all the barrage balloon cables were cut at once, the island would sink into the sea.

Up north, the bombastic Gen. George S. Patton seems to be busy preparing for the invasion across the channel near Calais. His tanks, trucks, guns, and supplies are not quite so well camouflaged. His security is just a bit lax as he swaggers about with his two pearl-handled pistols at his side and his shiny star-studded helmet. Here was the hero of the North African campaign; one to be watched, the Germans thought. Little did they suspect that his was a mission of deception. He was not intending to attack anything. Patton's trucks, tanks, and equipment were the world's largest collection of inflatable full-size toys—all fake, but quite convincing from the air.

Tonight, 28–29 April, an amazing drama will unfold, one of the best-kept secrets of the war. This is the tragedy of Operation Tiger, a large-scale training exercise off the south coast of England. The landing is to take place in the Slapton Sands area, whose beaches and cliffs are similar to the Normandy coast. This is the last and final test of all the skills required for the D-Day assault. Half a dozen LSTs, landing ship tanks, loaded with trucks, half-tracks, and tanks as well as thousands of U.S. Army 4th Infantry Division soldiers, pack the decks and holds of the ships as they cruise in line down the coast in calm, moonlit seas. The starboard side of the convoy is exposed because of an accident in Dartmouth Harbor the night before when an American LST rammed HMS *Scimitar*, assigned the vital task of screening this convoy. Nine German "E" boats on routine patrol find easy pickings as they encounter this armada on its unprotected starboard side. Three LSTs are hit and over 700 men and many trucks and tanks as well as other equipment slide into the sea. The burning oil and fuel are remembered forever after by those who lived along the coastal towns as "the night when the sea caught fire." All because *Scimitar*'s unavailability wasn't passed on to the proper command. This was just a little over six weeks before D-Day, when the 4th Division was slated to play a leading role. The mystery then was, and still is, how the Division managed to lose the better part of a regiment of men and equipment and not only keep it secret, but perform so effectively six weeks later in Normandy.

COME WITH ME TO A WAR

I
England

I turned to reply to General Palmer for the second time in the few minutes we had shared the rear seat of this British sedan. The first time the background for his head had been the typically well-manicured British hedge. This time he was about to become the grill ornament of a rather large military vehicle. Then came the crash! We had been broadsided. So began my tenure as aide de camp to Williston B. Palmer, Commanding General of the VII Corps Artillery. The accident report read: "Severe damage to right rear door of sedan." Irreparable damage to one general's dignity. The locale for this event was a British country estate surrounded by a labyrinth of tall hedges. The driver of our car, feeling quite important, with the flag of a general officer mounted and flying from the staff on his front fender, had taken off quite briskly and popped through the opening in the hedge as though he were the only driver on the road. He wasn't.

I had been a forward observer and an aerial observer with the 951st Field Artillery for a couple of years and was quite content. I had an excellent radio team of two men. We were certain that we would do a good job when our time came. Then came a notice for me to report to battalion headquarters. Lieutenant Colonel Isenberg, our battalion commander, advised me that Corps headquarters had requested the name of a second lieutenant with certain (unnamed) qualifications and that that individual was to report to Corps for a special assignment the next week. He made it sound as though it was something rather temporary. He further advised me that I was it. When the day came I found that the Colonel had made the battalion Piper Cub available to me for the 75-mile or so trip to Corps for an interview. I arrived at the country estate that Corps occupied to find that I was one of five lieutenants being interviewed for the position of aide to the Corps Artillery Commander, Brigadier General Williston B. Palmer. The Colonel and I were good friends and he wanted it to be a surprise, I guess.

We were interviewed in turn, and as I looked around the room, I could pick out at least three great candidates, each tall and very military. When I was called in to be interviewed by a friendly colonel, I was quite relaxed because I knew I didn't have a prayer of being selected. He inquired in detail about my military background, education, etc. He questioned me about some items of military history and military organization as well as current events. At last it was over. I was relieved that my pilot and I could make it back to our outfit, now located in the Duke of Norfolk's castle in Arendale, before dark. I didn't want to fly at dusk. With my thoughts on that subject, I was brought back to the present when the sergeant came out to call me in. The colonel who had done the interviewing said, "I must apologize, Lt. Maxey." This was a first. I had never had a colonel apologize to me. "The General is not here today to meet you. You will receive your orders to report here next week. Congratulations. You are General Palmer's new aide. Sergeant, you can inform the others that they can return to their units." I was one surprised guy.

When I finally met the General the next week, I was impressed with his appearance. Here was a stocky gentleman with a pronounced chisel chin which I told myself would precede both of us into battle. He wore steel-rimmed glasses and even when he smiled I had the feeling you didn't argue with this fellow. I felt fortunate that he was only a few inches taller than I and wouldn't spend all his time looking down to see where that 5'6" aide had gone! He was every inch a West Pointer and I liked him from the start.

I had encountered this man once before. I didn't think he remembered me at first, and I didn't recognize him as being the same general because our face-to-face encounter had been so brief. The 951st Field Artillery Battalion had been out on the English South Downs firing training problems when we had a "big brass" visit. This general came up on the hill that was serving as our observation post (O.P.). A narrow road ran along the back of this hill and it served as the runway for our field artillery observation planes. Our commanding officer, Lieutenant Colonel Isenberg, received the General, who turned and surveyed the valley and hills out in front of us and then turned to the colonel and said, "Colonel, see that line of shrubs out there about 1,000 yards beyond that rusty patch of grass?" The Colonel said, "Yes, sir." The General replied "That's a line of enemy tanks. Bring it under fire." The Colonel turned and looked at his officers and said, "Lieutenant Maxey, this is an aerial problem. It's yours." I was certain that I knew which line of bushes the General was talking about—well, almost sure—so I replied, "Yes, sir," and took off on a dead run down the hill shouting to my pilot, Lieutenant White, "Hit it, Whitey. We've got a fire mission." Whitey spun the prop on the little Piper Cub, climbed in with me, and we were off down the dirt-road runway and into the air. I was refolding my map and checking to verify the relative locations of the gun batteries and the O.P. I gave the range an estimate and tried to find the enemy tank location on the map. (The bushes weren't on the map.) I instructed Whitey where he should put us, clicked on the radio, and called range and direction to our guns, instructing them to fire one round HE (high explosive) fuse quick. I could hear the gunfire in the distance and I prayed that I had given the proper firing instructions and that the round would land in the vicinity—at least in England. England is such a small country. The Lord looks after fools and drunks and my first round was slightly long in range and to the left of the target by a couple hundred yards. I quickly gave the instructions to correct this and was pleased to see the next round 100 yards to the right and right on the beam for range. I could handle this and the enemy would never know what had hit him. I sent the proper commands over the radio and ordered another round closer to the target. It was right on. Following this I sent the command to fire the battery "for effect." The shells landed right on the "enemy tanks" and they were obliterated. I could see it now. I was going to be a real threat to the enemy in combat. Whitey and I circled around and landed on the little dirt runway. I could hardly wait to unstrap, get out, and run up the hill to receive my well-earned "well done." The General turned to me and said, "Fine problem, Lieutenant, wrong target." My Colonel told me later that the target identification had not been all that good. Targets seen from the ground can change drastically when seen from the air. I don't know why, but it never occurred to me to remind the General of our earlier encounter. I never was cut out to be a hero.

And now this was my first day. We were en route to the country estate being used as the Artillery Group headquarters for the final D-Day assault briefing of the artillery unit commanders. There were various levels of clearance, from confidential to secret to top secret, and then, for added security, only those with the need to know were given special scrutiny and referred to as "bigoted." On arrival, we all entered a large room, doors were closed, and guards were stationed outside windows and doors. The General unrolled a big wall map and proceeded to discuss the Corps' mission in the imminent invasion. He impressed upon his audience the absolute necessity for secrecy until their units had been loaded onto the LCTs and LSTs. He emphasized that absolutely no one who had not been bigoted was to share this information. I stood there in shock. I had heard all this. I had not been bigoted. I hadn't even been cleared for top secret. As a matter of fact, the cook wouldn't even give me his secret omelet recipe! I promised myself to sleep with my door locked that night and the window closed so that if I talked in my sleep I wouldn't divulge any of the secret information I had accidentally heard.

On the afternoon of the 4th of June, General Palmer called the entire staff to a meeting in the garden of the estate and had a friendly chat with us. He told us the invasion would take place in a matter of hours. I had already been briefed that it would be on the 5th of June. As we now know, it was delayed until the 6th of June. He gave a general outline of the location. He went to some length to assure that with the overwhelming force we were about to unleash, only the most extreme misfortune could cause failure. We were advised that as of that moment we were confined to our area except for official travel, and we were assigned vehicle numbers for the travel to Portsmouth when the word was given. As you would expect, the air was tense and the officers and men were silent for some moments. Each had his own mental picture of what was to come.

Within twenty-four hours our convoy left this area for Portsmouth and a huge, good meal under a shelter, and then onto assigned LCTs (landing craft tanks). We would have enjoyed this meal even more had we known that our food until we hit France would consist of canned split pea soup and bars of "jungle" chocolate meal after meal. Once in France it was K rations for a week and then split pea soup.

My boyhood dream of visiting France was about to be realized. I would have preferred a less rude approach. The thought of going into this treasure trove of art and culture with guns blazing struck me as the height of poor manners. Sort of like poorly trained firemen going into a mansion with muddy boots and fire axes to put out a wastebasket fire. I knew it had to be done, but it offended me.

The next day was the 5th of June, the original D-Day, and the invasion was delayed to the 6th. Our gun batteries were all loaded or en route to being loaded and all departed on schedule. Meanwhile, Corps Forward was boarding its transportation with leading elements destined to go ashore early in the game.

II

Utah Beach and the Capture of Cherbourg

In the historic assault on the European continent, 6 June, 1944, the VII Corps of the First U.S. Army was assigned to the extreme Allied right, charged with the mission of securing a beachhead on the Cotentin Peninsula, making contact with V Corps, First U.S. Army, on our left flank, and seizing the major port of Cherbourg as a base for future operations.

At about 0230 hours on 6 June, the first units of the Corps went into action when paratroopers of Maj. Gen. Matt Ridgway's 82nd Airborne Division began dropping astride the Merderet River and southeast of Ste. Mère Église, and Maj. Gen. Maxwell Taylor's 101st Airborne Division jumped in the coastal area. The 82nd Airborne Division captured Ste. Mère Église on D-Day, and the 101st Airborne Division took St. Martin de Varreville and Bouppeville, despite considerable difficulty because of the size of the area over which it dropped.

"Promptly executed the assigned mission" was the official Morning Report language. All very succinct. The whole story was much more dramatic. Beginning at 0230 hours, over 800 C47s dropped the jump battalions of the 101st and 82nd Airborne Divisions. They towed in hundreds of gliders loaded with troops, equipment, and supplies. These expendable one-way pieces of transportation littered the fields for miles around the beachhead area. Some were wrecked deliberately. The best way to bring them to a halt was to find two trees or buildings properly spaced and steer between them as one skidded across the fields, thus shearing off the wings. Some gliders were impaled on "Rommel's asparagus"—five foot stakes set in open fields.

The paratroopers were faced with the same difficulties plus more. I saw no gliders in the Caranton Swamp, but on D + 3 D + 4 I saw many parachutes hiding the bodies of our troopers loaded down with eighty to ninety pounds of ammunition, weapons, and equipment in the water. There were approximately twenty square miles of flooded area with some areas $1\frac{1}{2}$ miles in width. The wide dispersement of the paratroop drop was not planned. Pilots attempting to escape antiaircraft fire veered off course and dropped their charges as soon as possible. At a time like this, the paratroopers didn't need isolation. When I was in jump school I had heard stories of transport pilots going off course and dumping their troops anyplace just to get rid of them and get out. This was cowardice. One paratrooper told me that in Sicily his jump master was so enraged that before he left the door (he was the last man out) he pulled the pin on a grenade, tossed it toward the cockpit, and yelled, "Here you yellow————! Eat this!"

Following a heavy aerial and naval bombardment, at about 0630 hours, elements of the strongly reinforced 4th Infantry Division, now augmented by elements from other divisions, stormed the shell-torn Utah beaches led by the First Engineer Special Brigade. The 4th Cavalry Group seized the two key Iles St. Marcouf near the landing area. The Utah Beach assault casualties on D-Day (a little over 700) were approximately the same as suffered during "Operation Tiger."

By the end of 7 June the beachhead was firmly established. Our artillery had taken out the chief offending guns and the assault regiment of the 4th Infantry Division—the 8th Infantry—had driven inland to form a firm junction with the Airborne in the vicinity of Ste. Mère Église. Elsewhere on D + 1 our troops, in spite of heavy counterattacks, had passed Raveneville on the north and almost reached Azeville farther west. Meanwhile, engineers were organizing beach installations for the further buildup of the Corps troops.

By 8 June we of the VII Corps Artillery headquarters were waterborne, still some miles away from our destination on Utah Beach. Overhead, the traffic jam of planes was matched or exceeded only by the two-way seagoing traffic ferrying in fresh troops and supplies and bringing back the wounded. Some said that the boat traffic was so heavy you could just walk across the channel on them. This was not quite so. If the traffic had been that heavy, a lot of us would have attempted to walk back that first morning.

The next tragedy to hit the General was in the making. General Palmer was in the Corps Forward contingent and his Jeep and driver were on a different LCT. That LCT headed into shore late on D + 2, hit solid ground, and came to a halt. The door swung down and the driver and Jeep raced off. Problem: They were on a sandbar and the Jeep and driver disappeared in about six feet of water still some yards from dry land. The driver swam away. The coxswain, having dropped his anchor a short distance back, reeled in the anchor cable, pulling the boat back off the sandbar. He then gave it the gun, running over the sandbar and the General's Jeep—footlocker, bedroll, and all. I was certainly glad when I learned of this that I was on another LCT and not responsible for his equipment at this point. Amazingly enough, by the time I caught up with the General on D + 4, his equipment had been found and several men had been assigned the task of opening it up and drying it all out.

In the period 8–12 June the Corps expanded the bridgehead west of the Merderet River, securing a link with V Corps. The push in the north and northeast on the Quineville–le Mont de Lestre ridge continued for a week, driving the enemy back from the Neuville Plain and mopping up all resistance north of the Douve River and Canal au Pont de Carentan. So this action was in progress as we approached Utah Beach.

From Portsmouth to Utah Beach, the trip was a lonely one, to say the least. Those of the Corps staff on my LCT were friendly, but distant. I was the new guy on the block, having been with them for less than a week, and I was the aide to their commanding general, who himself had been with them only a short time. This was really not the time for light chatter. We had no time to find one another's common interests. The one thing we had in common was our concern for what lay ahead and even though we would have been the last to admit it, we were all damned well scared. We were headed into a situation over which we exercised absolutely no control. Our previous years of training now seemed to be as irrelevant as the phases of the moon. Fate was dumping us into an unknown hell. If you had a friend beside you, you could shore each other up and break the tension by idle chatter. If you were a stranger, as I was, you could only close off the outside world, pray, and dream of better times. I tried to visualize my wife, and tried to relive our days together and the love we had shared. We had been married only a little over two months when I left for overseas.

The "uniform of the day" was the standard GI fatigue outfit or work uniform impregnated with some sort of chemical that supposedly would protect us from gas in the event of a chemical attack. There was deep discussion about which of the two evils was the greater! The uniforms were stiff and smelly. To say they didn't improve with age in the next few days is at best an understatement.

I arrived on the beach early in the morning of D + 3 in our LCT loaded with light vehicles and members of the Corps and Corps Artillery headquarters staff. Occasional explosions of incoming shells from fortifications near Cherbourg rocked the beach, which was littered with wrecked equipment. I realized later on that being an artilleryman was an advantage. The sight and sound of incoming shells was less traumatic because of this familiarity. Nevertheless, one also had respect for the potential. As we watched an LCT take a hit while it was loading wounded we became a little more concerned about these shells. The shouted instructions of the beach master to "move it or lose it" took on serious implications. It was our heartfelt desire to get off that beach. Huge cuts had been carved into the beach embankment and our vehicles slowly clawed their way up the sandy makeshift roads and at last out of the beach area and away from the incoming shells.

Everywhere were lifesaver belts discarded by GIs as they came ashore. These inflatable belts carried a couple of gas cartridges. They were to be inflated in case of need. To activate the belt one only needed to grasp it at a certain point and squeeze. A pin punctured the tops of the gas cartridges and inflated the belts. Large sheet-metal tank breather ducts like those you would see in a big heating project lay strewn across the beach. They had enabled the tanks to come in through the water and then up onto dry land. Every now and then we saw the German mini-tanks, small-treaded, battery-powered vehicles about 18"x 18"x 24". These tanks carried bombs, and were guided by wires from German positions to destroy enemy targets. The debris of blown-up or wrecked vehicles and equipment was everywhere. As we got away from the beach we saw many parachutes hanging from the trees or left on the fields and numerous wrecked gliders, including those of American design and broken-up British Horsa gliders. I found it surprising that we saw no bodies—German or American—on the beach or in the beachhead area initially. Graves Registration cleaned up the immediate beachhead area quickly in those first days. This was not so a few days later, although American bodies were rarely seen farther than small-arms range from the front or in the immediate vicinity of a bomb or artillery attack. German bodies were not so quickly removed and the French got many pairs of new boots as a result. Barefooted German bodies were a common sight. At times, there was such an accumulation of blown-up equipment in the beachhead area that one wondered if there was enough left to fulfill our mission. Strange, how the sight of a German body seemed to have no emotional impact on me, but the sight of a dead GI at first left me almost nauseated.

We promptly headed inland to St. Mère Église. We spent the first night in an orchard in foxholes abandoned by the Germans. The Luftwaffe visited us off and on that first night as they did on succeeding nights. We had experienced them in England in the past few months, but this was more personal. They bombed our area quite thoroughly. The ground shook and dirt crumbled in around the sheet metal covered with sod over my head. I was quite certain that if I survived I would find a lot of the soldiers I had come ashore with gone by morning. Where would I find another Jeep? How would I contact General Palmer? At last dawn came and our planes took over the sky. My Jeep was still intact. The other members of my party came out of holes and basements. A runner came to take me to General Palmer and we were on our way! Succeeding bombing attacks found me much more optimistic. This was a good baptism. A damaged parachute hung in an apple tree near the foxhole where I spent my first night. I salvaged it and later brought it home. Another parachute draped a St. Mère Église church steeple about two blocks from me, and I later learned of the fate of that trooper. By playing dead, he had survived! The background noise was constant: gunfire in the distance, truck and tank motors close at hand. At night, antiaircraft fire with spent ammo raining down on the area created a definite hazard. Enemy aircraft were overhead from dusk till dawn. Artillery fire was the music to which we slept.

Mention should be made of the versatile $2\frac{1}{2}$-ton trucks that were modified to become amphibious. These trucks, known as ducks, did a yeoman's job during the invasion. They were loaded with men and supplies at shipside, then driven through the surf up onto the beach and to the supply dumps. They were a moving target and not easily sunk.

The Kraut air force had pretty well been chased from the daylight skies, but the nights belonged to them. Our bivouac area in the apple orchard bore evidence of this. Bomb craters abounded and you hoped that the odds were with you. We did lose a few people, but amazingly enough, not many.

The Corps command post was aboard a command ship held offshore for the first few days. The Corps Artillery command post was shortly moved to a set of stone farm buildings. The typical layout was a U plan of continuous construction with the dwelling an integral part of the whole. A lesson soon learned was to plan in the daylight the path on which you would run in the dark. You would be running to a foxhole in the case of an air attack or you would be running to a straddle trench to relieve yourself.

By fixing the path in your mind, you could avoid falling in that cattle manure pit in the courtyard. The French just don't do it the way we do!

Lieutenant Jack Weldon and I had served as enlisted men in the infantry medics early in our stateside training. I had left to go to artillery OCS in July 1942. Encountering him as an officer in the military police when I came ashore was a pleasant surprise tempered only by his first words. "Bill, glad to see you! I'm all shook up. I just had to investigate one of the damnedest things you ever saw. The body of one of our guys over here back of that shed. His pants are down to his ankles and he has a knife in his back. Don't be fooled into thinking all the enemy is out in front of you and in Kraut uniforms. Some of these French babes don't welcome us!" Well, that was fair warning and I treated the natives with caution after that. Days later, I saw armed FFI troops marching girls with heads shaved. These were suspected girlfriends of the Nazis. This situation was not surprising. Some of these German troops—young men—had been in the area for a couple of years. While the SS were to be feared, you could imagine a kid from Frankfurt was lonesome and feeling more like the victim of all this than the conqueror. The young Frenchmen were all off in prison or labor camps. The barmaid, the clerk in the bakery, or the milkmaid were equally lonesome and chemistry takes over and completes the story. When snipers were cleared from buildings as we went up the peninsula I saw now and then that they were female. This was, it seemed, a phenomenon of the peninsula. I neither saw nor heard of such incidents after the early days. You must also remember that after the first weeks we were being perceived as the winners and who wants to be caught sleeping with a loser?

It might be helpful at this point to understand where a

"corps" fits into the Army groundforces organization. In our case it all started with Eisenhower, *theater* commander in command of all forces in Europe and Africa. Under him was Bradley, commanding the 12th Army Group, with Montgomery as *ground forces commander.* Next, Hodges as *1st Army Commander* and Collins commanding *VII Corps.* Next in line of command were the various *divisions,* the *regiments,* the *battalions,* and the *companies.* The foregoing is an oversimplified picture of the command structure, but in order of command. The Air Force and the Navy were separate commands under Ike's wing. Most headquarters had a "forward" and a "rear" echelon. Thus, if the forward echelon was captured or bombed out, the rear could take over. I was always in VII Corps forward with the code name of "Jay Hawk." The first few days were spent planning position assignments for Corps medium artillery battalions when they would arrive. We needed more elbow room, and the infantry was busy providing it as they expanded the bridgehead. By D + 6, we were ready to welcome the much-needed 155mm howitzer battalions.

On the occasion of one of the early nights of shelling and bombing, I ducked into the lower level of an old stone building and found myself next to the Corps Artillery executive officer. He was the colonel who had interviewed me for the job of aide to the Corps Artillery commander. In the course of the evening I asked, "Colonel, why was it that you selected me in that interview for this job of aide to the General? Didn't I make it clear that I had no desire to be a general's aide? Because I never met an aide I liked." He laughed and said, "You know what, Lieutenant? I feel the same way. I have to work with whoever the aide is. I looked over the five fellows who were applying for this job. Four of them were panting for the position. I decided I liked the guy who wasn't really after it, and that was you. So, we'll see how we work together. I think it's going to be great." He was right, and I softened my stand on the subject as time went on. I learned to enjoy the assignment.

On 10 June, the 90th Infantry Division, elements of which began coming ashore on D-Day, was committed for the first time, passing through the bridge west of the Merderet with the mission of securing the Douve River. This division captured Pont l'Abbe on 12 June, the same day Airborne troops entered Carentan and a Regimental Combat Team of the 9th Infantry Division entered Criebec and Dangueville, while Montebourg was also surrounded. As these and other inland strongholds fell, stubborn coastal centers of resistance were cut off and reduced. This coastal drive ended on 14 June with the capture of Quineville and a line running along the road to Montebourg, but the 12th roughly marked the end of the second phase of the invasion, for by that date it was clear that the period during which a crisis might be expected was passed.

First blood! I was wounded a few nights after we landed and while we were still dug in at the orchard at the edge of St. Mère Église. The nightly enemy air sortie seemed to be over about midnight, and I jumped out without helmet for a trip to answer Mother Nature's call. As I returned to my foxhole, Jerry made one last pass for the night with guns blazing and our antiaircraft batteries answering. Out of the sky came a piece of hot metal right above my eyebrow. That was too close!

Even minor head wounds bleed like mad. Having been a medic, I knew what to do with this scratch. I taped it up, said a prayer of thanks, and went to sleep promising to wear my helmet in the future.

The next morning, General Palmer inquired about the

patch on my head. When I admitted what had happened, he said, "You should have gone to the medics and reported that. That's good for a Purple Heart." I replied, "Sir, if I have just missed my only chance in this war to get a Purple Heart, I will be most grateful." Besides, I couldn't imagine forever after answering the question "How did you get your Purple Heart?" with "Going to the toilet!" Life is full of hard choices.

Our helmets issued in 1942 were a blessed improvement over the World War I "pie tin" we had been issued in 1938. These new helmets came in two parts. First, the helmet liner of fiberglass with webbing designed to fit the head and absorb the shock from blows to the head. Over that was the versatile metal shell. This shell was a compromise between excessive weight and protection from shrapnel and other missiles. The ingenious GI soon found many other uses, such as a basin for washing and shaving, a mini-tub for bathing or laundry, a clumsy mallet for pounding tent stakes, a pot when he was stuck in a foxhole under enemy fire, and so on.

On the morning of 17 June, General Collins became curious about the seeming slowness of our Division troops in taking the city of Valognes, which straddled the main road from St. Mère Église to Cherbourg. He sent General Palmer (and his aide) from St. Mère Église in a Jeep to explore. Arriving in the outskirts of Valognes, it became obvious that the Germans were putting up stiff resistance. The streets were rubble-strewn and the enemy fired from the partially demolished buildings as our troops took one building at a time in costly fighting. Some of these snipers were German troops, but some were their girlfriends! We could only get partway through town. The Germans' "burp gun" fired a stream of shells that could cut a man in two. To see the wall close to you suddenly burst as these shells hit was intimidating, to say the least. One soon learned to wait for covering fire and then run or drive like hell past the exposed area.

This was our introduction to the odor of urban combat. The stench of burning human flesh and burning hair, added to burning clothing and furniture, was everywhere. We were to encounter this pungent odor in many villages and towns in the months to come. You felt stained on the inside after breathing this air, and the feeling wouldn't go away. The General determined that he still wanted to scout the front on our left to see if we were encountering resistance all along the line. Inching forward, we arrived at the road to Negreville to our left. The General relieved the driver of his duties and took over that job. He had been in this vicinity before the war and felt more confident in his own driving ability. We had to take evasive action to avoid sniper fire coming from upper floors of buildings. It was a rough ride, twisting and dodging down this rubble-strewn street. I could have used a seatbelt at this time. As we emerged from the town into the open countryside, I was sitting in the rear of the Jeep with the best view of the area. Suddenly, I saw a camouflaged German antiaircraft position in a field to our right front, with a camouflaged building for the gun crew dug into the ground at the far edge of the field. Soldiers were moving between this building and the gun position. I alerted the General, who immediately drove into a ditch along the road for cover. A hedgerow bordered the field, providing additional cover. The driver, the General, and I quickly dismounted and took up positions behind this hedgerow. On cue from the General we popped up above the hedgerow, waved our guns (the General and I each were equipped with .45 caliber pistols and the driver with a carbine), and yelled at the Germans to "Come on out of there, you bastards!" We moved back and forth to create the illusion of being more numerous and more dangerous than we were. Shortly, the antiaircraft gun was lowered, pointing in our direction. The General and I thought, *This is it*. We hunched down in the ditch, expecting fire in our direction, and extinction. Then silence. The gun elevated again and on it was a white pillowcase, or part of a white sheet. Surrender! Out they came across the field to us, helmets off, cloth caps on, hands in the air—twenty-one officers and men! We were well out in front of our forward elements. This would happen again as the months went by.

Once through the hedgerow and lined up on the road, the officer in charge made it known that he was highly embarrassed at having surrendered to three lightly armed Americans. He felt better when he learned that he had surrendered to a general officer. In broken English he then told us that he needed help with a wounded comrade back in their quarters. This could be a trap, and we all knew it! General Palmer had to make a decision; refuse to comply with the Captain's wishes, send the driver back with the Captain, go himself, or send his aide—me! As a humanitarian, he couldn't leave the wounded enemy. He sent me with the Captain. He didn't realize that inside my starched uniform beat the heart of a jellyfish! The long trip back up the road seemed to never end and as we turned into the field, I had the Captain on my left with my cocked pistol in my right hand, pointing across my body. I had such a firm grip on the gun that it is amazing it didn't go off accidentally. One unexpected motion from the Captain would have resulted in his immediate death.

It was dark in the hut—only the natural light from the door opening. Fortunately, the wounded soldier was close to the door. The Captain was probably more frightened than I by the apparent sound of multiple machine guns in the distance. In reality they were closer than he thought—my chattering teeth! I'll never tell! As you can imagine, all the while I was going up the road and into that belowground shelter, I took great comfort in the knowledge that if this was a trap and I was shot, the General would be very, very mad! I instructed the Captain to pick up his comrade and help him out of the shelter, and then we returned down the road to the rest of the troops. During this part of the operation I found that there was a well-camouflaged antitank gun in the ditch at the crest of the hill. We hadn't seen this and for some reason which only God knows, it wasn't manned at the moment we arrived on the scene. This was just the first of many occasions that at last convinced me that I really did have a guardian angel. All ended well. We marched our charges back to Valognes and turned them over to an antitank battalion. When we retraced our steps and continued on toward Negreville, we found that our recently captured gun positions had been under attack by our own troops all morning long from the opposite direction. Over the hill were American casualties, a burning Jeep, and a knocked-out Sherman tank! We were fortunate the enemy didn't see us coming and thought they were surrounded. "Never assume," we had been taught in OCS, and I guess it was true. Our troops had been on one side of the low hill, preparing to launch a new attack out of Negreville, while we were accepting the surrender on the opposite side. In a few moments, we would have been blanketed in our own artillery fire. General Palmer and I were decorated some months later for this action. We were each awarded the Croix de Guerre with palm leaf and bronze star and kissed on both cheeks by some French general with a smelly mustache! I could just hear those prisoners saying, "Let the punishment fit the crime!"

I came ashore well equipped for picture-taking. I had two whole rolls of film in my duffel. I realized later on that this was really being underequipped. I had been advised earlier that photographing in combat areas would not be allowed. This was not true, and I regretted many times that I didn't have more film. But, after all, photographing was not part of my job at first. As we progressed along the way, I obtained film from bombed-out photo shops and by courtesy of friends in the Signal Corps.

Days later, as we progressed up the peninsula toward Cherbourg, General Palmer insisted on joining the infantry point and walking up the road with them. You might think that the soldiers would appreciate the sight of a general officer walking with their squad or platoon leader, but such was not the case. Snipers were everywhere in the hamlets we passed, and we ducked into ditches or between buildings. A squad leader moved close to me on one occasion and pleaded, "Can't you get that brass out of here? He's just drawing fire and we don't need that!" As we reached an abandoned 88mm gun position on a hill, with ammo still burning and exploding, the General decided to stop and let the infantry continue on over the hill toward Cherbourg. The 88s had been spiked, fired, and demolished. (When it is the intention of a gun crew to destroy a gun to keep it from falling into enemy hands, a shell is rammed into the muzzle of the gun. The shell is pointing back into the barrel. A live shell is placed in the breach and the gun is fired, using a long lanyard for the sake of safety. This splits the end of the barrel, thus demolishing the gun.) As we stood on this hill we were the recipients of 88mm fire from a similar position farther toward town. These were air bursts and obviously coming from another six-gun battery. We, of course, hit the dirt with the first burst, the only shelter being the earth berms around the burning ammunition storage. After three salvos we made a run for it to get off the hill. As artillerymen, we scratched our heads. Three salvos and they still hadn't adjusted their fire to kill us! Obviously a poorly trained crew. They were firing from a fixed position and at a fixed position with no survey needed—all on familiar country—and still failed to accomplish their mission. Their problem was that the 88 is such a high velocity gun—really designed for antiaircraft—that it is difficult to cut the fuses with the accuracy needed for such a mission. It worked better for antiaircraft fire. This was amusing and frustrating too. Here we were, two trained artillerymen capable of knocking this battery out in short order, but with no phone or radio communication to our own artillery! We survived—good luck! We didn't take out the enemy—bad luck! Oh well, you win some and you lose some.

Clearing the debris of battle was a constant and gruesome task. The dead, bloated bodies of cows and horses littered many fields. The roadside ditches held the bodies of enemy and friendly troops, with the enemy being the last to be removed. Initially, our troops climbed over piles of masonry from collapsed buildings in the first push forward. They were followed by tanks with dozer blades, and as the snipers were cleared out, the regular road-building equipment proceeded. At times, a side street would escape almost untouched. Most civilians fled to the countryside, but others went to the cellars and lived through it or perished.

A most distasteful chore fell my way about a week after I landed. One of our men came to me with a strange request. He had been approached by a Frenchman whose horse had stepped on a mine. Would I please come and take a look? I accompanied him to the nearby farm, not knowing what I was supposed to do. When I arrived, I found the poor Frenchman in tears. This beautiful horse was on the ground with one leg blown off and a rag tied around the stub. Our conversation was in broken French, fractured English, and sign language, but we managed. The Frenchman explained that the horse had to be put out of its misery and he had no firearm to do the job. Besides that, he didn't have the heart. I was curious about how he had managed to keep this prize animal. The soldier said he didn't have the guts to do it either. I knew that the .45 caliber pistol I carried would do the job at close range and knock the poor thing out with one round between the eyes. What a strange way to enter combat. I took a deep breath, said, "Forgive me, Dobbin," and did the job.

Early in the game, our troops kept an eye open for German heavy-duty electric generators. These four-wheeled units were better than our units and served to light many a headquarters as we progressed along on the campaign. Captured German rations were a welcome change, too, from our K rations and C rations. We especially liked their canned white asparagus—grown in the dark and tender.

In order to prevent the reinforcement of the garrison at Cherbourg and likewise to forestall any orderly withdrawal of the enemy defenders of the port city, VII Corps undertook a third phase of operations designed to cut off the peninsula entirely.

At about this time I encountered Lt. Bob Evans. We had both volunteered from the 951st Field Artillery Battalion to join the 502nd Jump Battalion of the 101st Airborne Division, train in England, and jump in on D-Day to adjust Navy gunfire behind enemy lines. Bob had successfully completed his five qualifying jumps, but I had been one of several injured on our fourth jump. Mine was a back injury and knocked me out of the fifth and qualifying jump. Result, no paratroopers wings, and I was chagrined. Bob was a pre-med student before the war who volunteered for service—a great guy and a natural-born comedian. I was struck by his change in demeanor. His greeting to me was, "Bill, that accident that happened to you—you're better off in the field artillery. I wasn't on the ground ten minutes when I crept up behind a sentry, wrapped my arm around his neck, and killed him with my knife, just like we were trained to do. It was terrible! I will never forget it. It might be OK for some, but you and I aren't made this way. Don't worry about those damned wings you didn't get. You were lucky!" As time went by, I came to realize the wisdom of Bob's words.

The twenty field artillery officers who volunteered for that D-Day jump did so with the promise that we would be returned to our units right after the jump. Of the twenty, one refused to jump on his first training jump, and was kicked out of the plane on its third pass over the jump zone. Five, including myself, were injured on the fourth training jump, and three more on the night training jumps. That left eleven officers to head up as many radio teams on D-Day. Of the eleven, I was told four survived and found their team members and their equipment on the ground that morning. They were able to fulfill their mission and conduct fire.

Bob Evans's plane had been riddled with AA fire and the guys were anxious to get out. Bob had landed in a ditch on one side of a hedgerow and the remainder had landed on the other. To a man they were cut down with machine gun fire. Only Bob survived in these first few minutes, but Bob had been killed inside. I made contact with Bob again a few years after the war and realized the impact all this had had on him. This happy-go-lucky guy was now unsure of himself and could not continue with his education. He would never become a doctor, he said. I don't know what became of him.

The army reneged on its promise and kept all the survivors in the Airborne Division.

The 9th Infantry, veterans of Africa, attacked in the zone between the 90th (Tough Hombres) and 82nd (All-American) Airborne Divisions on 14 June. The Pont l'Abbe-Orglandes-Groubesville area had already caused considerable difficulty for the 90th Infantry Division, and the 9th Infantry Division met an initial rebuff in the same area. However, the drive across the peninsula began to gain momentum on the 16th. While the 90th Infantry captured Le Calais and the 82nd Airborne St. Sauveur le Vicomte, the 9th Infantry crossed the Douve River and drove rapidly across the peninsula in a push that carried twelve miles out to the north-south coastal highway at a point about three miles from Barneville-Sur-Mer. This was accomplished by 2300 hours of 17 June and thus closed off the Cotentin Peninsula, cutting a retreating German division in half and killing its commanding general. The commanding general of VII Corps transmitted to all troops a message of congratulations received from Field Marshal Montgomery for the Corps' brilliant performance.

To celebrate the cutting of the peninsula and the completion of that phase of the campaign, General Collins ordered the rations for our Corps headquarters to be turned over for one meal to a French restaurant staff—one of the few that had survived and one he knew by reputation. The staff then took our Spam and other delicacies and turned them into a gourmet meal—the only time during the campaign we had such a meal and oh, what a treat!

The speed with which the peninsula had been cut off made possible the rapid mounting of the fourth phase, the resumption of the drive on the original Corps objective: Cherbourg. On 19 June, three infantry divisions, the 4th, 79th, and 9th, attacked abreast. The 4th Division cleared Montebourg and attacked to seize the high ground north of the town. The 79th Division, after passing through the 90th Infantry Division, jumped off to capture the dominating terrain northwest of Valognes. The 9th Division advanced rapidly to the north and elements of the attached 4th Cavalry advanced to within four miles of Cherbourg on the southwest.

Property accountability is a real fetish in the Army and an officer's career could rise or at worst fall on his ability to remain correctly accountable for all of the thousands of articles listed in his "property record book." I knew of one officer whose record book was in the worst possible shape. I had participated in the inspection of his unit before we left England. A couple of weeks after the landing I met him and he had a great big smile on his face. I asked the reason for the smile and he said, "Bill, you wouldn't believe the sad thing that happened to me. A small case I was carrying with my property record book in it was lost overboard in the Channel! That's not so bad, but I'll sure miss my good luck stone that was in the same bag."

On 20 June, a ring was drawn around Cherbourg's outer defenses by our speedily moving infantry units. Valognes was captured after strong resistance from fortified positions on the high ground. The 9th Division likewise met prepared defensive positions southeast of Flottemanville-Hague. Weather precluded any aerial support of our advancing GIs. The General and I felt pretty proud that we had contributed by eliminating that antitank, antiaircraft position a few days earlier.

Cherbourg was surrounded on 21 June and advancing elements cut the road leading to St. Pierre-Église Road. All divisions continued to envelop the defense of the Fortress Cherbourg, but the German commander refused to surrender. An aerial bombardment preceded an attack by all three divisions the next day, and despite strong resistance, the city's outer defenses were penetrated.

Prisoners (POWs) from Normandy came in small groups at first and then in droves and they were marched back to the beach and shipped over to England, then transshipped to the United States. England had all the mouths to feed that it could tolerate. As the Cherbourg Peninsula was cut off, the POW flow increased and the burden of guarding and caring for these people became a major task in logistics. Getting them off the peninsula, on boats, and out of our hair took on a serious priority. While they were recognized as the enemy, I rarely saw them maltreated—only a little rough now and then. From D-Day to the end of that first month we took a total of over 33,000 prisoners (including our twenty-one).

Living in England for several months prior to the invasion had provided some unexpected training: life in blackout. This is a phenomenon that cannot be described; it has to be experienced. As we moved about during the invasion and the drive through France we never saw lights from farm buildings or houses and certainly never from vehicles on the road. Only "cats' eyes." After months of experiencing this, one became acclimated and it all seemed quite natural.

The attack was continued through 23 June with substantial gains by all units. The 79th Infantry Division broke through to within one mile of the city. The advance through the fortified zone continued the next day, knocking out pillbox after pillbox. On 25 June all divisions advanced to the outer edge of Cherbourg. Small units entered the city, and captured all major forts in close-in defense of the fortress. All of Cherbourg except the arsenal was in our hands on 26 June, the day that Lt. Gen. Dietrick von Schlieben, the garrison commander, and Admiral Hennecke surrendered to us. I recall the haughty and arrogant attitude of this general and admiral as we brought them into the courtyard in front of our headquarters. Sitting there in their high-peaked caps and leather long-coats, they attempted to act as though they were accepting our surrender instead of vice versa. They were allowed to stay in the open command car for quite some time and after a while they became very, very restless. They stood up, moved around as best they could inside the car, and sat down again. Suddenly it occurred to me that General Collins was allowing them to roast a little bit before taking them on and turning them over to authorities to transport back to England. It worked quite well. After half an hour or so they began to look a little bit less haughty and a little bit more defeated. And those of us standing in the courtyard armed and waiting for them to try something funny were amused by the entire situation.

During this phase of the campaign the FOBs (Field Artillery Observation Battalions) gained their durable reputation. The function of these units was to pinpoint the source of enemy fire, thus providing our artillery with targets. In turn, our artillery, 155mm Howitzers and 155mm and 8-inch guns, regularly knocked them out, sight unseen. Their method of operation was basically as follows: A ground survey was conducted along our front, accurately locating as many observation posts (such as church steeples, water towers, tall buildings, and hilltops) as possible. Our artillery was then tied into these locations by survey. Microphones were placed in each of these locations, as was an aiming device such as a BC scope tied into the baseline and pointed toward the enemy. Sound and flash gave the enemy away, and day or night, these units, by triangulation, gave information to our guns and counter-battery fire was quickly conducted. It was rare when enemy fire lasted long enough to do appreciable damage or disturb our sleep. The FOBs were unsung heroes.

Our artillery conduct of fire is one developed by the Prussian army. It calls for, among other things, firing four gun batteries as a unit with one gun firing test rounds to verify range and direction from the gun to the target, with the guns out of sight of their target, and then the battery "firing for effect." Batteries in turn are tied together by accurate survey in such a manner that a battery has its firing data firmed up, allowing the battalion of twelve or more guns to be brought to bear on the same target. This was devastating enough, but another refinement is added called TOT—Time On Target. By the use, once again, of accurate survey data and the information from that first lone gun placing a round on or near the target, the range from all guns in the vicinity to the target is calculated as is the time of flight from gun to target. Wind, powder temperature, and distance all enter into a formula for quick calculation. The result is the capability of firing an infinite number of guns twelve, twenty-four, sixty, with all shells arriving at exactly the same moment. No warning shells, just total devastation. This is most demoralizing and later proved a factor in demolishing the defenses of Aachen as well as other targets of opportunity. The Prussians invented it, the Americans perfected it and used it, and the Germans ignored it, preferring to use their high velocity 88mm guns as direct-fire weapons and the Stuka dive bomber to place the explosives on the target. The Stuka was a dumb weapon, easily knocked out once it faced trained antiaircraft troops who had overcome the fear of this weapon. With the Allied mastery of the air, the Stuka was left in the garage.

German heavy and medium artillery were encountered, of course, and were very effective. The basic problem was that it was rare to find guns in quantity, and frequently it seemed they were short on ammunition. They didn't seem to follow up after scoring a target hit. Unlike the Russians, they didn't employ mass artillery. We were always thankful for this.

As the enemy pulled out of the Cherbourg Peninsula, some unusual incidents took place. In one such case, a large contingent of the enemy selected a small sunken country road running parallel to our front. They assumed that they had gotten far enough ahead of us to be safe and not retreat in line with our troops. The road was bordered by five-foot-high hedges, thus affording still additional cover. Unfortunately for them, our aggressive artillery commanders, having found no enemy resistance on their front, moved ahead of the infantry in the local situation. As the guns were being put in place a short distance back from this sunken road, sounds of approaching traffic came down the road some distance to the battery's right flank. Hurried investigation resulted in the discovery of an approaching, slow-moving enemy column including tanks, trucks, horse-drawn equipment, and supply wagons. The battalion commander ordered the gun placement to be hastily completed. The guns were set to fire horizontally, and blind, through the roadside hedge now some 150 yards to our front. A field telephone was run to the commander's left flank with an observer hidden in the hedges ahead of the column. When the column had pretty well transitted the width of our front, hidden from view by hedges, the commander ordered all guns to fire several rounds. The observer reported total demolition of the tanks, which were unable to return fire because they couldn't traverse their guns. The embankment and the hedges they had coveted for cover became their prison and their shroud. The guns were the long-barreled 75s and were so long-barreled they could not be turned because of the high banks on each side. Our infantry came up and cleaned up the job.

Immediately after the brief battle and surrender, the survivors were taken prisoner and voluntarily organized themselves into work teams. They pulled the dead from the tanks and other vehicles, assembled the wounded and gave them first aid, then made ready to be marched off. I was impressed with their discipline.

It was not my style to go around picking the bones of enemy dead, but as the smoke died down from the burning tanks and ammunition, I walked cautiously down the road. I found a P-38 pistol in the holster of one officer and it looked to be in usable shape—he wasn't! I brought that home as one of my few souvenirs.

From time to time, a chicken would fall in the ditch and break its neck. The only thing to do was to find a clean helmet and cook the poor thing. This was done from time to time. It was forbidden to just go out and kill local livestock of any kind for our use—so, of course, we could only enjoy "roadkill." Better than the K rations!

As we advanced we occasionally overran units and

individual enemy soldiers who were trapped behind our lines. Some were snipers left in buildings or in trees. These gave us a deadly surprise when we stopped advancing for the day and set up our field kitchens for chow or found a spot to roll out our blankets for the night, only to hear that nasty bee-sting sound of a rifle shot or a grease gun and see, if you were lucky, only one or two men drop. Then the urgent task at hand was to locate the sniper before dark and take him out.

On other occasions, enemy soldiers were left behind by accident and hid out in farm buildings and hedgerows, wanting to rejoin their units or just survive, not certain they could surrender and live. It was disconcerting to roll out in the morning only to find that you had spent the night only a few feet from the enemy on the other side of a hedgerow! I was one of several who spent one night snuggled up to a hedgerow, rolled out in the morning and headed for the chow line, heard a fuss behind me and turned to see one of our guys flush a Kraut out of the other side of the hedge.

Incidents of this sort were many and many of them humorous. Night convoys of trucks met enemy convoys, joined them for several miles, and then parted to go their separate ways without realizing what had happened until later. Everything was in blackout and no one could identify the vehicle next to him.

For days on end, we lived and slept in our uniforms. When the quartermaster finally provided laundry services, we felt we were being rejuvenated. We were in our wool uniforms after we took off the anti-gas, impregnated uniforms, and took advantage of white gasoline for dry cleaning when it was available. Smoking was done with great care at these times.

Both sides, but particularly the enemy, used mines of various kinds throughout the war. Mines and booby traps were of limited value to an aggressive army on the move like ours. They are more for defensive purposes. The 9-pound Teller mines took their toll when mine-clearing activity could not keep up with our lead elements. These mines could pulverize a Jeep, wreck a heavy truck, or take the track off a tank and/or roll it over. You soon learned to stay on the road and not drive around a stalled vehicle onto the shoulder. Walking in the fields was equally deadly because of the so-called "shoe mines" and the "bouncing Betty" mines that proliferated in some areas. These mines could all be cleared by our minesweeper engineers. The most effective minefields were those where the enemy could observe them and cover the area with machine gun or small arms fire. In this manner, they could keep us from digging and clearing. The methodical Germans usually laid out the minefields according to a plan and kept accurate records of their locations, and so it was vitally important that we capture those plans. As much as possible, tanks equipped with "flails" (rotating drums fitted with lengths of heavy chain that beat the ground) exploded the mines and cleared the way. These were a British invention. The engineer who removed these mines occasionally found them to be booby trapped. If he was fortunate, the discovery was to his benefit, not just to his buddies. Mine removal is still World War I–style: stick the bayonet into the soil, find the mine, uncover it with your hands, identify it for type and size, dig around it and lift it out. Defuse it, but first feel under it for booby traps.

By 27 June, Cherbourg and all the peninsula except portions of Cap de la Hague were occupied. The arsenal surrendered at 0940 hours. The only resistance elsewhere was in the outer harbor ring of forts. Ile Pelee, one of the forts in the harbor, capitulated 28 June, and the following day the remaining harbor defenses, Fort de l'Est, Fort Central, and Fort de l'Ouest ran up the white flag.

We devoted several days of each week to inspection of our field artillery battalions and their gun positions. General Palmer would check on such items as clean ammunition, proper positioning of the shells and powder charges in the individual gun positions, camouflage, relative positioning of the guns in relation to each other, and good housekeeping. Shells must be clean if they are to function properly and not foul up the firing mechanism in the guns. Powder charges for our guns must be protected from the elements and possible accidental ignition. The medium and heavy artillery have separate powder charges in silk bags. Guns must be positioned so that the muzzle blast from one does not cause discomfort or injury to the crew of a neighboring gun. Premature shell bursts as the projectile leaves the gun do occur on rare occasions and can kill the neighboring gun crew. Good housekeeping goes with good morale. Proper sanitation is a concern of all good officers who care for the health of their troops.

I have indicated before my lack of enthusiasm for becoming a general's aide. I had encountered several who were overly impressed with their own importance and it had disgusted me. I had run into one such young officer during training in the States. His general had since passed away and this fellow had become a battery officer. By coincidence I now found him in command of a battery we were inspecting. He met our Jeep as we arrived with all due pomp and immediately started trying to impress the General with his background as an aide to a general. As we inspected the gun position—which was not perfect, but not too bad—I could sense the General was getting fed up with his constant self-praise. We prepared to leave and I went ahead to get the Jeep and the driver. As I went through two parallel rows of shrubs I suddenly looked to my right and observed the most disgusting sight. The shrubs on either side bordered an old wagon trail. The personnel had used the space in between them as a toilet as well as a garbage dump for all manner of refuse. No attempt had been made to dig in and cover up. Most unmilitary! I stopped in my tracks and turned to face the General and the still-chattering lieutenant. The General said, "Go ahead, Bill, get the car. I'm through." I just nodded and smiled and looked over my shoulder. This was all General Palmer needed. As he followed my gaze his face got red, as did the lieutenant's. The lieutenant's well-prepared efforts to impress the General melted in the next few moments as he was lectured on sanitation. I had seen this guy get many of my fellow officers in trouble over very minor infractions of the rules in the States. Now this was one for them! As time went on, I met many aides who were fine officers and did not fit the biased image I had developed. The ADCs serving General Collins were tops.

My old unit, the 951st Field Artillery Battalion, was a fine outfit. I had trained with them since January 1943 in the States and in England. The General was impressed with them. On the occasion of our second inspection visit in the field he turned to me as we rode away in our Jeep and commented, "Goddammit, Bill, you came from a first-class outfit. You should be proud of them!" What the good General didn't know was this: I got the list of battalions to be inspected the night before, in order to set up the routes. I would take the driver and Jeep out in the evening, grab the Colonel from our outfit, tell him what specific points the "Old Man" was pounding on currently, and then do a brief inspection on our own. Nothing like a little preparation! Nothing like taking care of your old buddies!

The next two days, 30 June and 1 July, found the last enemy resistance in the Cap de la Hague peninsula mopped up, bringing to a close this remarkable campaign in which the Corps spearheaded the assault that cracked Hitler's Atlantic wall and gained a strong base in Fortress Europe for subsequent operations. In these twenty-six days of operations more than 39,000 enemies were captured. Even more important, the way had been cleared for an unlimited drive into the enemy's vital inland areas.

Before the POWs from ETO (European Theater of Operation) were sent to the U.S. we were told that there were already 425,000 in camps there. These were the result of the African campaign.

My younger sister was employed by the phone company when I left home. I recall a letter from her telling me that she was now with the Douglas Aircraft plant in Chicago and was making $1.05 an hour! Can you imagine? A girl making such a fabulous wage? I thought about this for some time. She had advised me that she didn't feel part of the war effort just sitting at a switchboard. She moved from our small town to Chicago for that reason. The war had an impact on the whole family. Mom went back into teaching when the drafting of men created a teacher shortage. Dad came out of retirement and utilized his equestrian background by becoming a mounted guard at a local ordinance plant and my eleven-year-old brother, Don, did close-order drill with his BB gun in our backyard. I could tell from the letters that my mother and my wife suffered the most anxiety of all during this period.

Thousands of rubber contraceptives were supplied to the troops and many found the expected use, you can bet. The innovative GI also found other uses. It was worth a chuckle to see other weapons—i.e. rifles, machine guns, and similar caliber weapons—sporting these protective devices on the end of the muzzles as tanks, half-tracks, and trucks roared down the road. They did a fine job of keeping the moisture out and didn't have to be removed in case of a sudden need to fire the weapon.

III

The Hedgerow Fighting

The period from July 2nd to 24th may well be called the period of the "hedgerow" fighting, and was as bitter and costly as any participated in by Allied troops in the European operation. This period was almost entirely an infantry-artillery duel on terrain that afforded the enemy almost ideal defensive opportunities.

The average Normandy field, hemmed by hedgerows, was the size of an American football field. In one aerial photograph covering 7.6 square miles, over 3,900 of these tiny, hedge-enclosed fields and orchards were counted. Ingenious GIs from Ordinance came to the rescue by welding long V-shaped steel teeth on the front of our tanks. The tankers then raced across the fields and rammed holes through the hedge bases. It was a great sight, but the tankers told me they were taking a bit of punishment too. What a surprise for the Nazis dug in on the opposite side of the hedgerow! Up until this point in time, our tank would have ridden up on the hedgerow berm, pointed its nose into the air and exposed its vulnerable belly. The German soldier would calmly fire their version of our bazooka, called a panzerfaust and very effective, into the underbelly of the tank and mark up one more kill. Now, after a short period of "education" seeing their fellow men buried in their gun positions, the Germans hit the road when they saw a tank headed in their direction.

Mail is almost as vital as food to a soldier. You know

that all sorts of things can delay delivery. Nevertheless, when you see your fellow men getting mail and you have gone for some time without, your morale takes a hit. Changing units, as I had done just prior to the invasion, goofed up my mail. I expected some delay and was all set to accept that fact. Then on 6 July, after no mail for over a month, I was told that mail for me had been seen in one of the Corps offices and I was elated—two letters and a *Reader's Digest!* When I went to that office no one could tell me anything about it. I lost my cool and raised hell with the office staff. I was getting the brush-off and I didn't like it! General Palmer overheard my tirade and came to investigate. I was embarrassed and apologized for my loss of temper. General Palmer said, "Don't apologize! This is an unacceptable hell of a note! I want this place searched right now!" Wastebaskets, boxes, and bags were all turned out, but no mail. Next day it showed up in the mail and my temperature returned to normal. My wife, Eva, wrote faithfully almost every day while I was overseas. She was teaching at Green Bay High School in Green Bay, Wisconsin, and seemed always to find some newsworthy subject to cover. General Palmer had a chuckle after the mail arrived one day. It seems his lady friend had sent him a small package containing those hard-to-get ladies' silk hose. Included in the package was a note wishing him well and admonishing him to give these away "one at a time."

By 24 July the Corps had pushed forward in the swampy, inundated area south of Carentan to the general line of the St. Lo-Perriers Road. This was the front line for Operation "Cobra" which was to find the VII Corps breaking out of Normandy and spearheading the First U.S. Army's great drive that was to liberate Paris and sweep on through the historic Meuse-Marne-Aisne River country to

Belgium and the Siegfried Line. The brunt of this hedgerow fighting was borne by the 4th, 9th, and 83rd Infantry Divisions. An example of the intensity of the hedgerow fighting is indicated by the fact that the 83rd Division alone suffered 1,391 casualties in one afternoon. I found it very depressing as the reports came in.

As we broke out of the hedgerow country, tanks, Jeeps, and armored cars were buried under blankets of flowers and apples as we went through the towns and countryside—you could see the natives running down the lanes and over the fields toward the highway as the lead vehicles went forward, the vehicles all laden with armloads of cut flowers. They would toss apples into the open vehicles. General Palmer thought this was great until, standing up in his armored car accepting the accolades of the crowds as we sped through one town, his head arrived at 40 miles per hour at a particular point in space coincidental with a tossed apple. It caught him between the eyes! Comes time for a policy change. All future accolades will be acknowledged from a less exposed position—sitting down! He was quite fortunate, really. I had heard that our troops in Italy were welcomed by grateful and enthusiastic Italians throwing huge bundles of ripe grapes into their tanks and trucks. These became instant grape juice on the fronts of the uniforms and before the day was out, an attractive target for flies. As our army moved up out of the vineyard district, other items were to be thrown in welcoming the liberators, including amaryllis stalks. These weighed up to four pounds and proved to be deadly when they came in contact with the hero soldiers.

When we rode close to the lead tank, which at times looked as though it were part of a homecoming parade with bundles of flowers everywhere, we suddenly heard machine guns chattering and saw a rain of flowers explode off the tanks as they met resistance and went into action. The atmosphere went from festive to deadly in less time than it takes to read this. In a moment, the citizens all disappeared in houses and barns or behind stone walls.

It was exhilarating to be free of the hedgerows and the secrets they held. You never knew for sure that the enemy had been cleared on your right or left as you sped down a road. Moving out in the country with larger fields was more to our liking. We all felt ready for the major effort that was being planned. Concern over possible gas attack was high as the invasion took place, and continued for several weeks. As time went by the concern lessened and gas mask carriers started filling up with apples, cigarettes, and other items. Gas masks themselves found their way into the duffel bags and settled to the bottom.

Given these circumstances, we were ill-prepared when a German fighter strafed our Corps Headquarters in a little hamlet one night just as we had settled down for a good night's rest for the first time in days. One building was a barn built of stone and clay. As luck would have it, a truck with a load of phosphorous shells was parked next to the barn and it caught a few rounds. The truck exploded, and the shells lit up the sky. The explosion shattered the clay barn, sending great clouds of dust into the air, and this witch's brew with the light from the shells convinced some poor lieutenant that the resulting cloud was a gas attack.

The lieutenant and his driver started down the road shouting "Gas! Gas! Gas!" I was on the second floor of a small building, dug into the barracks bag for my mask, and after a few minutes decided I couldn't find the damn thing and just went out into the yard to see what was going on. At this moment General Collins came out of the house next door in his pajamas and bathrobe. He shouted to the guard to "get ahold of that idiot shouting the alarm and bring him back to me." So off sped a Jeep with a couple of MPs to find this alarmist. Well, he was found and brought back. By this time General Collins had lost a half hour's precious sleep, was cold from standing in the middle of the road in his night clothes, and angrier than I had ever or did ever see him. He gave that lieutenant a lecture on verifying his information before sounding such an alarm and sent him back along the road to yell, "All clear. All clear. All clear," in both directions from our command post—first east and then west along the front of two divisions. Then he said, "Once you have covered that, do it again!" As I drifted off to sleep I still could hear that poor guy passing by on his rounds calling, "All clear. All clear." Our intelligence was pretty conclusive to the effect that the Germans had no intention of using gas. We found no evidence of stockpiling near the front. Additionally, we had air superiority and a much greater delivery capability for retaliation.

IV

The Breakthrough

Following the greatest aerial bombardment in the history of warfare by more than 3,000 planes, elements of the 9th, 4th, and 30th Infantry Divisions jumped off in that order from right to left on 25 July in a push that was to result in the Marigny (wrongly called St. Lo) breakthrough. The St. Lo-Coutances Road was a major highway and was looked upon as a fine visual bomb boundary line for the Air Force to use. Unfortunately, three quarters of the way through the planned bombing program, the smoke and dust had billowed up to a cloud over a thousand feet high and had drifted over this highway, obscuring it from sight at altitude. This resulted in the bombers mistakenly using a similar highway running at an angle—the St. Lô-Perriers Road—as their bomb line. The established twelve-hundred-yard safety zone was violated and our own positions came under attack.

General Palmer and I set out to inspect our artillery positions along the front and visit some battery and battalion command posts in the vicinity of Le Hommet. We became aware as we drove along that the sound of explosions and the shocks of the concussion waves were getting uncomfortably close. Amid the dust and smoke we could see nothing alarming. Out of the haze as we approached it, a cluster of masonry farm buildings, which we identified as our destination by the military vehicles parked around them, exploded in a cloud of debris. A direct hit by a cluster of bombs from the B-17s had wiped out an artillery battalion headquarters, complete with staff, wire trucks, kitchen trucks, transport trucks, and all. We knew those people and were horrified. All we could do was notify their next higher headquarters and call for help. So much for "saturation bombing." This technique was used again, but with limited results as the official report states. A vast quantity of munitions was used by the Air Force in "saturation" bombing, but every square foot of ground does not merit this punishment, because every square foot does not shelter the enemy. Artillery placed on the target is much more effective on a pound-for-pound basis. The French must still be digging bombs out of their fields of sugar beets, and we didn't even declare war on their sugar beets.

Piper Cub airplanes used by the field artillery for observation and control of fire flew like dragonflies through the day, directing fire from division and Corps units. Everything from 75mm guns to 105mm, 155mm, and 8-inch guns was involved. Amazing as it may seem, these little Piper Cubs carrying a crew of two—i.e., pilot and an artillery lieutenant observer—on occasion could command the artillery punch of a destroyer. No wonder the enemy tried so hard to shoot them out of the sky.

The official records said that "limited gains" were made immediately after the bombing attack. This at a time when we expected that the enemy would be dazed or demoralized or even dead. We were wrong. We learned an important lesson this day: well-trained, dug-in troops can withstand this sort of an attack and still respond. Only by protracted denial of support—communications, food, medical and munitions supplies can a determined enemy be definitively destroyed.

All tank destroyer units and antiaircraft guns not required to perform their primary mission reinforced the mass fires of the field artillery preparation that preceded the attack and furnished continuous supporting fire. Planes of the Corps Artillery provided counter-flak air control and continuous counter-battery surveillance in the Corps zone of action.

As previously stated, the bomb line was the St. Lô-Perriers Road, and despite the fact that our front line units had withdrawn 1,200 yards, bombs dropped short caused more than 600 casualties, principally among the 120th Infantry (30th Division) and 3rd Battalion, 47th Infantry (9th Division). Among those killed was Lt. Gen. Lesley J. McNair, who until shortly prior to that time had been Army Ground Forces Commander.

Units of the right and center divisions pushed ahead about 3.5 kilometers while left flank units registered gains of two kilometers against stubborn tank-infantry-artillery resistance. The next day the Corps threw in its armored might as the two flank divisions peeled off and held open the gap. The 8th Infantry continued to spearhead the 4th Division drive, and Combat Command Boudinot of the 3rd Armored and the 1st Infantry Division passed through the 9th Infantry Division. The remainder of the 3rd Armored passed through the 4th Division, and the 2nd Armored with Regimental Combat Team 22 (4th Infantry Division) attacked through the 30th Infantry Division. This technique of having units in reserve pass through front line units, like the teeth of a comb, was an effective technique. It allowed battle-weary units to hold a position until relieved by fresh troops without disruption or loss of position to the enemy.

All units made good progress and by nightfall of 26 July enemy resistance was largely broken in the Marigny area. Even so, the enemy fought back for every yard of the way. Marigny and the high ground west of the town were held; elements entered St. Gilles, had a firm grip on that place and the east-west road through the town, and also reached the railroad just north of Canisy. A blown bridge halted armored units north of the town, but infantry pushed forward 2,200 yards south of Canisy, an advance of 8 kilometers. As can be seen, our carpet bombing did not roll out the red carpet for our infantry.

The collar badge worn by a general's aide is a conventional shield with red and white vertical stripes topped by a blue horizontal field. In that field are one or more stars depending on the rank of the general to whom one is assigned. On occasion, when addressing others, it is assumed you speak with the voice and the authority of the general. It behooves you personally to use the greatest of discretion on all occasions. If you overstep your authority too frequently, you become the local S.O.B. If you are reluctant to step up to bat when the occasion merits it, you are not an effective right arm to your general.

The one "hot button" with General Palmer was stalled traffic on the roads. A stalled column is vulnerable to surprise attack by enemy left behind in the villages or in forests. It is vulnerable to air attack. It is obviously not accomplishing its mission and more importantly, it is keeping my General from his mission of the day! It was my habit to leave the Jeep on the run when I saw we were being held up and keep going until I found the source of the blockage. Once I had made that determination I would start directing traffic and clearing up the situation. On one such occasion I found two colonels at a road junction with their two converging columns and each standing his ground on priority. I listened for a few minutes then stepped up with my aide's badge showing prominently on my collar and my Corps (higher headquarters) patch on my jacket being obvious. I saluted smartly and said, "Excuse me, gentlemen, the General has been stuck in this column for ten minutes. He is very disturbed at this situation. May I suggest you find a solution—quickly?" As I saluted again and walked away they found a solution and I met General Palmer's Jeep moving toward me at a good pace. On occasion, one can shout very quietly!

As we drove from unit to unit for inspections or conferences the General usually managed to just coincidentally hit a Division Headquarters at lunchtime and be invited to have lunch with one of his old West Point buddies. I was included on most occasions and so became acquainted with some of the top brass. On other occasions this caught us in the middle of our planned coverage for this day or the plans were altered at the last minute and I had the task of revising or expanding the route plan I had so carefully made early that morning. I then had no time for lunch or socializing. I spent my lunchtime picking routes, asking questions, and memorizing checkpoints, which would all result in getting the General where he wanted to go in the shortest time and with the least amount of mileage. Being alert to information regarding enemy-held areas was also part of the assignment. However, the Old Man all too often insisted on using his own judgment in this area. Nevertheless, frequently, as I was finalizing my preparations for the afternoon portion of our trip, General Palmer would show up full and happy, bidding his host good-bye and ready to roar off. I was left to fight the map and my notes in the windy back seat of the open Jeep. I would open a K ration and nibble as I could—at times in some rather grisly surroundings. This was especially true on hot days when bloated bodies of farm animals and/or enemy soldiers abounded. I remember on one occasion in particular when my well-fed General turned around in his seat and exclaimed, "Goddammit, Bill, you eat your meals in the damnedest places!"

One of the items of equipment issued to our forces fairly late in our pre-invasion training period was the full-track prime mover (towing vehicle), designed to tow the 155mm howitzer, the 155 long tom and 8-inch howitzer. This replaced a fine piece of equipment—the 5-ton diamond T truck—and added still more mobility to the artillery battalions. These were Corps and Army items. Another latecomer was the self-propelled 105mm howitzer issued to divisions to replace and improve the towed units used up to this time. These guns were mounted on a modified Sherman tank chassis and added greatly to the speed and mobility of division artillery. They were known as the "Priests."

An amusing, but frightening, incident took place one day as General Palmer and I drove toward our forward elements. We began to meet soldiers on foot hurrying toward the rear—singly, in pairs, and then in groups. After a few minutes we hailed a sergeant and asked for an explanation. He replied, "Oh my God, sir, tanks are breaking through and coming up the hill toward us and we don't have anything to stop them!" The General said, "Where are your officers, soldier?" The soldier replied, "At battalion officers call, sir." The General thought for a moment and instructed the frightened sergeant to get into our Jeep, and we drove on forward. We encountered more panic. We stopped on a knoll, got out the field glasses, and identified the "enemy tanks." They were in fact our own Priests. We then found the battalion officers call located and alerted them to the situation. The Priests had inadvertently sped through our forward positions, realized the error of their ways, and were returning. Fortunately, they encountered no enemy and very fortunately our spooked troops had no antitank weapons available at the moment. This was a frightening situation. An alert enemy would have exploited this soft spot in our lines and should have been following these frightened troops right in our faces.

By 27 July the enemy's positions were completely overrun, and by evening we had reached Coutances, although isolated pockets of resistance remained to be mopped up. The German 130th Panzer "Lehr" and 5th Paratrooper Divisions were badly smashed. The latter continued to fight in traditional paratrooper style, and its engineer battalion was wiped out almost to a man after a fanatical stand.

As we followed the main route of advance, General Palmer frequently decided to explore the countryside on our flanks. I always had a feeling that the good General had never heard of "curiosity killed the cat." One morning we took such a side trip and encountered a strange sight. There was a complex of masonry buildings, which had been some sort of an institution and was situated in a woods. An explosion of some considerable force had taken place here and the trees were stripped of small branches. Everywhere the ground was littered with unexploded shells—artillery, antiaircraft, and belt ammunition. Broken crates of mines were strewn about.

Some of the buildings seemed to be intact, with only their windows missing. There were no signs of life. As the General directed the driver to drive through this eerie mess, I decided that I should get ready for action, just in case one of those buildings held a welcoming party. Sitting in the rear of the Jeep, I pulled out my trusty .45 and put a shell in the chamber. At the sound of this action, the General went up off his seat about six inches and turned to see what I had seen. When I explained that I was just taking precautions, he said, "Goddammit Bill! Don't ever do that again!" The truth was that he was as uptight as I. We finally threaded our way through and out of this exploded ammunition dump.

A major asset for the VII Corps was its leadership at the top. Those of us privileged to work with General Collins, General Palmer, and the other top staff officers grew to recognize the quality of these men as they were put to the test time after time. They were firm, but fair. No posturing in the style of General Patton. Just the business of conducting the war day after day. Always aggressive, but also always a great concern for the lives and welfare of the troops. General Bradley and General Hodges were of the same ilk.

General Collins had made a reputation for himself in the Pacific, which resulted in his being selected by Bradley to command the VII Corps in Europe when it was formed. In turn, the various top staff officers had distinguished themselves in the Pacific or in Africa and were known personally or by reputation to General Collins. So it can be seen that the "team" commanding an Army, Corps, and Division is rarely assembled by chance, They are classmates at the Point, friends, acquaintances, or at least known by reputation. This has always been true in the service. General Grant named nine of his card club friends from Galena, Illinois, to be generals in the Civil War. General Pershing named his fellow lawyer from Lincoln, Nebraska, Charles Gates Dawes, to be a general in charge of supply transportation in France during World War I, and so it goes.

One entire company of our troops, bivouacked in the woods one night, heard activity in another part of the woods, and assumed it to be friendly troops. Chow was finished and they bedded down for the night. Next morning they realized the sounds were not all that familiar; in fact, the commands were distinctly German. They organized an attack from a standing position and killed or captured the enemy unit.

A great experience is map reading and driving under pressure in a foreign country. I knew no French, so names which were similar became the same at first glance. Added to this situation was the necessity of reading and directing the driver "on the fly"—that is, as we barreled down the road. Sitting in the rear of an open Jeep, with wind always, dust frequently, and rain from time to time, was a real challenge. I must say that I misdirected the driver only a couple of times and the General was most forgiving on these occasions. Fortunately, they were only of minor consequence and I soon learned to be sure to read "Canisy" and "Cerisy" as well as understanding that a "St. ___" has significance—with it is one town, without it is quite a different town. The French had "saints" all over the place. The strain was terrific.

Resistance during 28 July consisted mainly of strong rear guard forces left behind to protect and keep open the enemy escape route around Coutances. St. Denis le Gast fell. Other armored elements enveloped the strong enemy position at Montpinchon.

Air Force claims were a bit of a thorn in the sides of the ground forces throughout the war. I heard many complaints. As I traveled by small liaison planes to gather information, I observed an almost laughable phenomena. Sure, railroad yards were put out of action and towns were damaged seriously, but out in the country where road junctions, bridges, and road/railroad intersections were the intended bullseyes, the countryside was littered with bomb craters. In many cases it seems the safest place to park would have been on the bullseye—that is, the road junction. Bomb craters were all over the countryside.

I found it amusing to visit Air Force fields and be shown their charts (they were great for charts) and be told of the tons of bombs delivered on the various targets. They were very extravagant with their bombs and yet had minimum effect, in some cases, on the targets.

I don't recall the regiment or the commander's name, but General Palmer and I arrived at their command post in the woods one morning to find an air of great excitement and a lot of nervous laughter. They took us to their dug-in command post, all covered with logs and dirt. It all looked quite secure. They then escorted us to where their commanding officer had opted to spend the night. It was a nasty hole in the ground with shredded bedroll and clothing all about. It seems their Colonel had decided he didn't want to spend the night underground "like some animal." He opted for an open trench in the ground. The chances of a shell or bomb hitting that small opening were "very, very slight," he said. Well, a bit after midnight, Mother Nature called and the good Colonel crawled out and headed for the facilities in the woods—the straddle trench. Some Kraut fly-boy selected that precise time to fly over and drop a bomb in that woods. Bullseye! A random bomb landed in the Colonel's trench! The Colonel laughed and laughed, then he cried. That was too damned close. That cost him some new uniforms and a replacement bedroll. He didn't eat prunes for a week!

Trip wires were strung across paths and roads on occasion throughout the combat area. These were connected to antitank or antipersonnel mines. Our tanks soon took on an extra "skin" composed of sand bags laid on the sloping front side of each tank to make up for the vulnerability of our armor to the German 88mm guns.

Booby traps abounded—explosive pens, flashlights, cameras, and briquettes of pressed coal left in farmhouses.

As we drove toward Coutances in the late afternoon of the 27th, General Palmer examined the contour map and identified a small hill off the main road. He decided we should take a back road, climb the hill, and determine what we could see in the direction of Coutances. We found the hill in an isolated area, parked the driver and Jeep off the road in a small field, and climbed up. There was a structure up ahead that looked like a silo—about 20 feet in diameter and 40- to 50-feet high, constructed of fieldstone. As we ascended the hill, we heard a noise back down on the road and turned to observe three German Volkswagens loaded with soldiers being accompanied by a motorcycle with sidecar, all going down the road in one heck of a hurry. They didn't see our driver and Jeep in the field and certainly didn't see us climbing through the brush on the hill. They had apparently been left behind in one of those pockets. The military version of the Volkswagen was their Jeep. It was a boxy little five-passenger vehicle. It was powered by the same little air-cooled motor we later came to know so well here at home. As we climbed the hill, we found the vegetation had all been burned off around the silo. The sun came out and our map made a nice target for some alert observer. We got four or five quick rounds from some light artillery placed down in the valley. I hit the ground with the first round and got a nice black uniform out of it from the charred grass. The General had been closer to the silo when the first round hit. We scampered behind the stone silo and then, after waiting a while, down the hill. We had seen all we wanted to see for one day. This was too close for comfort and was getting to be a bad habit. There was much more to come in the months ahead.

Only later did we analyze the situation. How come a 75mm gun instead of the high-velocity 88mm gun? Of course. These were our own tanks firing at us! We were in enemy territory and being fired upon by so-called friendly troops! We had failed to watch the phone wires in the ditches. When you run out of phone lines you are most probably past the front lines!

Our Jeep—or later our armored scout car—was plainly marked with the red plate and the General's star. Further, the white letters read VII CORPS HEADQUARTERS. While this frequently gave us "the right of way," it also had disadvantages. The GIs would not take the responsibility of stopping our vehicle and telling us to turn back because we were headed into enemy territory. They assumed any general officer from higher headquarters knew more than they did about the situation. Obviously not always so!

That evening the General called me into his quarters to have a little conference. He said, "Bill, I want you to get rid of that driver." I was quite shocked because I couldn't see why and indicated such. He replied, "He's bad luck. You remember, he's the fella that was driving when we had our first accident in England; he was driving when my footlocker and bedroll got run over in the ocean; he was driving when we got out ahead of the front lines in Valognes; he was driving on several other occasions when we got in a close shave; and he was driving today. I want a new driver tomorrow." I was a little surprised at this and then I realized that General Palmer actually was a bit on the superstitious side. He felt that this fellow was bringing us bad luck. It was my opinion that the liaison section had not given us adequate information on enemy positions, and that was why we were having some of these problems. Nevertheless, before the evening was out, I had arranged for us to have a new driver and we kept him for some time. The thought that this driver did bring bad luck was supported, however, by the fact that within a week, while chauffeuring a captain in the combat area, he was captured, and the two of them were missing for two and a half to three months until we picked them up in a prisoner's cage down the line. Maybe the General was right.

General Palmer's buddy from West Point days was a big bear of a man by the name of Col. Bill Bullock. He was a full colonel commanding a Field Artillery Observation Battalion. Around corps headquarters he was known as "Big Bill." General Palmer developed the habit of prefacing his remarks to me with "Well, Goddammit, Bill, let's get out there and see what's going on with this outfit," etc. All this to the point that the staff got to referring to me as "Goddammit Bill" and to Bullock as "Big Bill." I had no idea that the General was aware of this until, years later, I received a letter from him in which he jokingly called me "Goddammit Bill."

General Palmer's Jeep was ordered to have a steel box under the back seat (where I sat). This box was about 10"–12" high and held a few K rations, clips for the tommy gun, and some powerful binoculars, which were booty from one of the German coastal gun installations. This box was very convenient, but it lifted me up for a great view of the surrounding countryside—and put my head above the hedgerows on each side. In this deadly game, where a low silhouette is a life-saving goal, the German snipers must have laughed at my head buzzing along just over the top of the hedgerows. I rode many miles with my back hunched down.

Following the original breakthrough between St. Gilles and Marigny, the two flank divisions peeled off to hold the flanks and keep the gap open for our exploiting armored-infantry teams. By the 29th, the enemy was trapped under increasing pressure exerted by the 2nd Armored blocking his escape southeastward by holding a line that extended from St. Denis le Gast to Lengronne and the Seine River. While elements of the VII Corps checked enemy movements in other directions from Coutances, the 3rd Armored and 1st Infantry Divisions hammered the enemy thus trapped from the west, northwest, and north, raking him with murderous fire as fighter-bombers pounded him from the sky.

I always enjoyed working with the "Big Red One," the 1st Division. When General Palmer and I encountered them in the early morning hours and later as liaison officer when I crossed paths with their units, I was struck by the importance they placed on food for all of their troops. Their seemingly impossible goal was fresh eggs for everyone every morning.

The Division had established a budget for egg purchase. Further, they had created an "egg patrol" composed of officers and enlisted men who daily scoured the countryside for eggs—sometimes up front, but as we advanced, to our rear. I enjoyed the fruits of their labor whenever possible. Cholesterol? What is that?

On a hill southeast of Coutances, the General and I got

out of our Jeep and crept along forward to the crest to observe a pitched battle going on down below. The Germans were doing a stubborn retreat, firing as they went. It was certainly a time to keep our heads down, which we were doing. I was on one side of the road and the General was on the other, using his field glasses. Suddenly I became aware of the fact that we had company. A fellow in dark dress was creeping up on the General, and reaching out for him. It was too late to warn him. As this fellow tugged at General Palmer's sleeve, Palmer jumped like he'd been shot. In one swift motion, the guy reached into his jacket pocket and produced a bottle of wine and a glass. He just wanted to make us welcome. General Palmer accepted. He needed it!

Elements of the 4th Division were dispatched to help the 2nd Armored Division hold its long line and prevent enemy infiltration. The St. Denis le Gast-Coutances-Montpinchon area was choked with enemy vehicles and armor trying to escape, and the carnage heaped upon them by the VII Corps was unsurpassed on the Western front. Casualties inflicted by the 2nd Armored Division alone totaled 4,500, with 500 vehicles destroyed. Our Air Force claimed 137 tanks destroyed in addition to 57 damaged and more than 500 other vehicles knocked out.

By the end of July the Corps had advanced some 40 to 50 kilometers and burst completely clear of the Cotentin Peninsula's base. Terrific casualties were inflicted on the enemy in both personnel and materiel. The Germans lost more than 2,500 vehicles, including 600 tanks.

As I traveled throughout the peninsula and viewed this destruction, I couldn't help but think of the waste of all this—the material as well as the lives lost. The hours of labor all this represented. What a shame the German leaders couldn't see fit to put all this to work to build a peaceful nation. Then I could have stayed home!

VII Corps had paved the way for First U.S. Army's subsequent remarkable "Blitz," a blitz that carried through France and Belgium into Germany and also made possible the employment of additional American armies.

An enlisted man—usually one who is on the less rugged side—is frequently selected to be a personal assistant to a general or senior officer. This man is known in the jargon of the service as the "dog robber." He cares for the general's clothing, shoes, bedding, etc. General Palmer's dog robber was a slight little fellow of Latin American descent. He was a very pleasant guy and quite efficient. He was a great crap shooter in his spare time. The word was out that he was a force with the cubes to be reckoned with. I was told by others who had been on the ship with this fella coming to England from the States that he methodically worked through the hold of the ship, one deck at a time, cleaning as he went. By the time he reached England, he was a fairly well-off soldier. His problem was that there was a limit of, I think, $350 that an enlisted man could send back home. (I think the limit was predicated on a percentage of the individual's base pay.) This innovative guy paid off officers to send money back home for him, and it worked.

I was very fortunate to be in a headquarters unit, in many ways. In almost all cases, water supply was set up in trailer tanks in our headquarters area. Immersion heaters were placed in GI cans and when you found your room, corner, hole in the ground, or whatever for the night, you could go to this central spot and dip out some nice hot water—fill your helmet and enjoy a "bath." A shave. A bit of laundry. Because from barns to chateaux, utilities were apt to have been destroyed. This was routine. As in all units, food was cooked in portable "field kitchens" carried in two-and-one-half-ton trucks. It was possible to cook right in the trucks, but most cooks preferred to take their heavy 2' x 2' x 4 $\frac{1}{2}$' units out and work outside of the truck.

We were on the move as we traversed France. We moved daily. I was usually up early preparing route maps for the General and would witness the frantic efforts of our cooks preparing breakfast, cooking ahead for lunch on the road, and getting ready to break camp for the next move. They were the unsung heroes. In combat units they had a different task. They cooked food and packed it in thermal packs or insulated aluminum containers that required two men to lug them to a Jeep and then to armored columns or by hand to a sheltered spot near the so-called front lines. The cooks' helpers and the first-aid men were the bravest and most selfless men in the field on many occasions—it's difficult to carry a rifle, and use it, while lugging a food pack or a wounded body.

Near Alençon in France, we bivouacked in a large apple orchard in farm country. It seemed safe at last to pitch a pup tent and relax for the night. I had been asleep for only a short time when I heard our driver call me in a hushed voice, "Lieutenant, Lieutenant Maxey." I thought, "Now what? Surely the General is asleep; he was turning in when I left him." I answered the driver's call, lifted the flap of my tent, and there he was in the semi-darkness with a large drinking glass full of milk. He said, "Here, sir. This is fresh from the cow and still warm. It's great!" Well, I had to admit it was a real treat. Then I realized he was not alone. Off to one side stood a female. The driver said, "That's not all. This is Jeanette and she is anxious to make us happy. You can have her for a while, then I'll come back. I'm sleeping in the house with her tonight."

Well, I thanked him for his thoughtfulness, refused the invitation, spent the next two minutes wondering if I had made the wise decision, and went back to sleep. A phenomenon of France was the availability of intimate female company as we passed along. I later heard tales several times that once the war was over and officers and men retraced their routes, the picture had changed, much to their chagrin. The liaisons they thought they had established through one- and two-night stands on the way to Germany vanished upon return. The answer frequently was, "But, Monsieur, there is a difference. The war, it is over." Having just been married I felt the moral obligation of my vows. That was one restraint. A second restraint was the result of the months I had spent as a medic with the 129th Infantry. I saw firsthand the sad results of promiscuity. It was frightening.

V

The Great Defensive Battle of Mortain

The first week of August found the Corps further exploiting its previous success, and by 7 August elements were holding the high ground east of Mortain. To the southeast, Mayenne had been occupied, and armored elements had reached Domfront. It was on this day, 4 August, that the Germans launched their great counteroffensive to drive a wedge between the fast-moving First U.S. Army and the Third U.S. Army then moving down the coast on the axis of Mortain-Avranches in a major drive to the sea. The brunt of the enemy thrust fell on VII Corps and the 30th Old Hickory Infantry Division in particular. The enemy struck in the greatest strength he had yet mustered on the western front in the early hours of morning and achieved some initial success. His main effort was in the vicinity of Mortain and the area east of Cherence le Roussel. The enemy infiltrated into the area around St. Barthélemy in addition to Mortain and Roussel. Although the penetration was contained by the Corps and the counterattack halted, the Germans succeeded in isolating one battalion, 2nd Battalion of the 120th Infantry 30th Division, east of Mortain. The atmosphere at Corps headquarters was very tense. Both at our command post and on the road, we found ourselves under artillery and occasional small arms fire. It was a reminder, if we needed one, that this war was far from over. All efforts to regain contact with the battalion failed until two minutes before noon on 12 August. The courageous stand of this battalion in holding this key terrain feature in the face of all types of enemy attacks for more than five days gained them the sobriquet of "The Lost Battalion of World War II."

To aid in stemming the German attack, the 4th Division was rushed from reserve positions into action, and the 35th Infantry Division was attached and assigned the Mortain-Teilluel sector. Elements of the 3rd Armored Division were attached to the 30th Division and the First Infantry Division, which repelled enemy attacks in the vicinity of Mayenne. The 2nd Armored Division moved to attack German assembly areas in the vicinity of Barenton. The 30th Division was engaged throughout the day by the enemy's determined attacks, while the 9th Infantry Division was in fierce action. The Germans made a successful penetration in the rear of the 39th Infantry Regiment and other elements from the east toward Le Mesnil Tove on August 6th and 7th. The other two regiments of the 9th Division attacked to relieve pressure on the 39th Infantry, and by noon had gained the road east out of St. Michel de Montjoie. They crossed the east-west road to Gathemo also, and liberated l'Aubiere.

This was a frightening period as General Palmer and I scurried from unit to unit, consulting with division commanders and ordering repositioning of artillery battalions in order to support the infantry most effectively.

On 8 August the Corps continued to consolidate defensive positions and withstood all enemy attacks, eliminating infiltrators. The 30th Infantry Division severed enemy penetrations in the vicinity of Le Mesnil Tove and re-established the defensive line: Barthélemy-Romagny. The veteran 1st Infantry Division held firm against all enemy thrusts. The 35th Infantry Division attacked to relieve pressure on the 30th Division and made limited gains until held up southwest of Mortain. Small gains also were made by the

9th Infantry Division against very stubborn opposition. While the 4th Division held defensive positions, the 2nd Armored attacked in two columns and made good progress.

The morning of 9 August, Corps was getting those messages which indicated that some areas of the front were lagging. I am not certain of the designation of the division involved. General Collins and General Palmer and their trusty aides set off by armored car for a look-see of the front. We inadvertently bypassed the Division Headquarters. We couldn't find the Regimental headquarters and wound up with the forward elements. We walked the last half mile, arriving at a long ridge. Soldiers were crouched in the heat and dirt behind the ridge and every now and then first-aid men would drag a wounded or dead GI through an opening back to this shelter while small arms fire ripped the air over our heads. The unit was stalemated. Scared, hot, and tired. The generals inquired about the presence of the officers and were told, "The Lieutenant was killed this morning and the officers to the right and left are at officers' call back at Regimental headquarters. We are afraid the Krauts are getting ready for an attack, from what we can hear and see." Collins and Palmer were enraged at this poor judgment in leaving these soldiers leaderless. We made our way back to the rear and found the Division CP (command post). As we pulled into this farmyard we saw a large van-type vehicle off to one side. There was a platform about three feet off the ground and wooden stairs to it. As we pulled to a halt right in front of this platform, the door of the van opened slowly and out stepped the Division Commanding General in a lovely colored bathrobe, toweling his freshly shampooed hair and facing two hot, dirty, disgusted generals. One his boss! That general would have gladly gotten down and rolled in the dirt if it would have "leveled the playing field"! In a few minutes, with some well-chosen words, Collins humiliated that man, explained his job to him, gave him directions on just what he expected him to do in the next hour in chapter and in verse and gave him more than a brief peek at his probable career future. The General's Division progressed that afternoon and within a few days was doing well under a new Division Commander.

Renewing the attack to eliminate the enemy threat from the east on 9 August, the Corps met determined resistance but inflicted heavy casualties on the enemy. The enemy showed no inclination to give up the ground southwest of Mortain without a struggle. However, by 10 August the 35th Infantry Division had reached the outskirts of the town. Meanwhile, the 30th Division had failed to gain contact with its 2nd Battalion, 120th Infantry Regiment. The drive of the 2nd Armored Division was delayed by an enemy counterattack. Other units held defensive positions with elements of the 4th Infantry Division in reserve.

On 11 August the 35th Division reached its objective along the Mortain-Barenton Road, but it was not until 1158 hours on 12 August that "The Lost Battalion" was relieved by its own 30th Division elements. Meanwhile, the attacks of the 2nd Armored Division and 9th Infantry Division had shattered the enemy's hopes of cutting off the two American armies, and he began pulling out. By the close of the period the Corps was regrouping for pursuit and the part it was to play in the Falaise Gap.

VI

The Falaise Gap and Rapid Move to the Seine

The remainder of August found the Corps participating in the series of rapid moves of all Allied forces that resulted in the Falaise Gap and the subsequent series of envelopments that cut off ever-increasing numbers of the enemy west of the Seine River. To give the devil his due, the enemy did largely succeed in extracting the bulk of his forces across the Seine, but his losses in materiel were terrific, and by the end of the month VII Corps alone had taken a grand total of 60,000 prisoners of war.

Operating under the Corps at that time were the 1st, 4th, and 9th Infantry Divisions and the 3rd Armored Division, which had begun to come into its own and gained for itself the name "the Spearhead Division." Certainly the Spearhead and the "Hell on Wheels" 2nd Armored Division were the two most powerful armored juggernauts that operated in the west in the European campaign.

General Palmer held great admiration for General Maurice Rose, Commander of the 3rd Armored Division, and we traveled with units of this division from time to time. This was a risky undertaking, as these were very aggressive troops and well led. The objective was to observe their reaction to German resistance firsthand. I came to realize that career officers needed these opportunities to be in harm's way to earn some decorations for their tunics if they wanted a promotion. I wasn't interested in promotions—only survival. We seemed to attract fire on too many occasions and I took very little comfort from overhearing a conversation between General Palmer and General Rose after a particularly active day, when they were discussing a fellow general's career. The one phrase that struck me was, "You know, between Africa and here, Jim has had three aides shot out from under him." I began to feel like a cavalry horse.

On 13 August the Corps attacked to the northeast and met very little opposition as armored elements advanced 40 kilometers to reach Ranes. The veteran 1st Infantry Division reached the road between Juvigny and Couptrain. Other units regrouped.

Fairly heavy fighting developed on 14 August. Enemy resistance centered around Ranes, and the 3rd Armored Division was engaged in that vicinity throughout the period. However, elements of the 1st Infantry Division captured Le Ferte Mace. On this division's left, elements met more stubborn resistance but captured Juvigny. Meanwhile, the 9th Infantry Division moved into attack positions between 3rd Armored on the right and the 1st Infantry Division on the left. The 4th Division remained in Corps reserve and performed maintenance and rehabilitation after more than two months of almost continuous fighting.

As we drove from unit to unit one day, we met a Jeep and van headed in our direction. The Jeep, driver, and one passenger were all quite conventional, but the other front seat passenger was quite extraordinary. She was blond and very friendly as she waved and smiled. What a pleasant sight. We stopped at the next road junction to talk with the lone MP on duty there. He was quite emotional when General Palmer asked who that was we had just met. "That was Dinah Shore, sir! You know what, sir? She stopped and stood up in her Jeep and sang two songs just for me! Then she asked for a request, and sang that too. Isn't that just great, sir?" As he finished he had tears in his eyes. He was the happiest soldier I had seen in a long time.

General Collins consistently ordered the forward party to seek out the best location and accommodations for the Corps headquarters. His theory was that his staff operated more efficiently and thereby to the benefit of all subordinate units, right down to the foot soldier, if they were working in decent surroundings. Many other commanders theorized that they had to work under canvas, wading in mud and snow, sharing the hardships of the soldier to keep his loyalty. Collins' theory paid off for all. Admittedly, some days we spent in a barn, some in houses, some in chateaux, but always the best we could find. We passed one night in France in a large country home that had been the World War I headquarters of the American First Infantry Division. The Big Red One was still carved into the mantel.

Stubborn resistance continued on 15 August at the Corps' right, especially in the Ranes-Vieux Pont area where the enemy fought a determined rear-guard action. The 9th Infantry Division commenced its attack on this date with two regiments abreast but was able to make only small gains. This was the case also with the 3rd Armored. The 1st Division consolidated its previously won positions.

Many of the French villages we passed through had narrow streets and they were frequently lined with cheering villagers. As we raced ahead traveling in the armored columns, my morale was at a peak. With each kilometer, I felt that we were one kilometer closer to home and my bride. This couldn't go fast enough. Then sad things took place: The tank ahead of us slid sidewise as it negotiated a curve in a street at high speed and an old fellow had his foot run over. His neighbors were screaming at the tank and pulling him back. The day before, we had been traveling in our armored scout car when two lovely French girls were waving to us enthusiastically. The scout car had quarter-inch rods with little metal flags welded to the outer edge to aid the driver in gauging the outer limits of his vehicle. The girls didn't see the rods and as we reached them at high speed, one of the girls waved her arm over the sloping side of the car and was caught by the rod and thrown head over heels to the ditch. These things sickened me and I thought how even the most innocent suffered from our actions. We could not stop to help and could do little to prevent such incidents. The sight of that girl in a heap in the ditch and that poor old Frenchman with a smashed foot stayed with me for days.

The main effort of the 3rd Armored was directed toward the left (west) on 16 August to secure the high ground and road centers of Ecouche-Putanges (the towns exclusive), southwest of the Orne River. These objectives were achieved, and the gains consolidated. An advance of about ten kilometers made by Combat Command Hickey, a special unit of the 3rd Armored Division, which saw the division fight its way out of Ranes and north to Fromentel. It was a fight all the way, however, and at the end of the day they were heavily engaged in the latter town. Then the hard-fighting, aggressive 9th Division advanced two to three kilometers, seizing the objective, a prominent hill. Other units drove the enemy out of Mangy Le Desert, and seized objectives in the vicinity of La Vannerie.

Fromentel continued to be the scene of bitter opposition for the 3rd Division on 17 August, and two task forces commenced flanking movements to the left and right to come in on the enemy forces north of Fromentel. The 9th Division completed occupation of objectives with elements along the La Bouronniere-L'Angle Cherie road and southeast of Briouze, while other units were in reserve. At the end of the day the 9th Division was not in contact with the enemy. The 60th Regimental Combat Team was operating with the 3rd Armored. The First Division continued to hold, and the 4th Division remained in reserve. The withdrawal of the Germans and subsequent advance of the British cut off the First Division from enemy contact.

What is a task force? It is a unit formed by selecting armored elements—that is tanks and half-tracks and antitank artillery, as well as antiaircraft units, special infantry units, and so on. This made-up unit is trained and drilled to fight under one commander. It is normally less than regiment in size, very mobile, and not encumbered by support or housekeeping units. Its mission is to deliver a Sunday punch.

Final remnants of resistance within the 3rd Armored zone were mopped up north of the Fromentel-Ecouche Road on 18 August. By the next day, mopping-up operations were completed in the Trieze-Sainte-Batilly area, and all other units of the Corps were out of contact with the enemy. "Mopping up" is a phrase used frequently as sort of a catch-all for minor actions. If, however, you are personally involved, "mopping up" can mean one hell of a battle. Injured or dead is the same to the individual in all cases. The telegram reads the same.

As a high school student, I had contemplated seeing Mont St. Michel, that 13th century fortified monastery located on an island west of Avranches. It was on my agenda of things to see, along with a list of French Gothic cathedrals. Reading of the devastation the war had brought on similar places and monuments in Italy, I feared that I would probably find them all a pile of rubble. My high school principal was also the school French teacher. She had two-by-three-foot photograph posters of Mont St. Michel, the Cathedral at Chartres, and others mounted high on the wall of our study hall, and they fascinated me. I was greatly pleased when General Palmer planned a side trip to a hill near Avranches just to be able to see Mont St. Michel. By great good fortune, the Germans decided not to fight for it and it escaped. Later I arranged an unauthorized Piper Cub flight out at the time when the tide was out, and landed in front of Mont St. Michel on the sand. It was great sport.

Now we approached another gem right on our route of advance—Chartres. This was the most perfectly proportioned of all Gothic sanctuaries, I had been told. Additionally, its windows were of incomparable and irreplaceable 13th-century stained glass. Would my luck hold out? Would I get to see this, or would I only see its ruins? Then, on the 23rd of August, word came that an informal delegation of citizens from Chartres had come to us. They told an amazing story. Upon learning that our forces were nearing their town, the citizens had armed themselves with makeshift weapons from their barns, shops, and kitchens, and overpowered the German garrison. The town was open and no action was required on our part to take it. The cathedral would be spared.

This was all very good news and I enjoyed visiting the cathedral on the 24th, but where was the spectacular 13th-century stained glass? It had all been removed many months before, crated and stored in the crypt below the sanctuary. I would have to come again to enjoy the sight of that glass.

Many of us contemplated our arrival in Paris with great anticipation. We hoped that the city would be spared the fighting and bombing that had been the fate of other cities. It was with more than a little envy that we received the word that the 4th Division had been designated to represent us as security detail for Paris and that the French, who had had only a minor role in all this liberation effort, were to enter as the heroes. The net result was a rather subdued acknowledgment in the field that Paris was indeed liberated. We hated to admit it, but it made sense psychologically and politically to handle it all that way. Nevertheless, we had other work to do and so the Corps shifted to the south and bypassed Paris, continuing on with the job while the French troops and the rest of the world celebrated.

After a reconnaissance by the 4th Cavalry Group along the Seine River between Corbeil and Melun on 25 August, elements of the 3rd Armored began crossing the historic streams late in the afternoon. The Corps drive to the northeast gained about 35 kilometers east on the Seine the next day, with the 3rd Armored spearheading the advance and the 4th Cavalry Group screening to the northeast of the armor. The 9th and 1st Infantry Divisions followed on the right and left of the armor, respectively, and moved to assembly areas west of the Seine, crossing the river on 27 August. That day the Corps advanced 25 kilometers with the 3rd Armored crossing the Marne River at Le Ferte Sous Jouarre and west of Meaux. The cavalry was engaged in mopping up south of the Marne.

August 28th found the spearhead 3rd Armored advancing 45 kilometers, capturing the historic towns where some of World War I's greatest fighting took place—Soissons, Chateau-Thierry, and Braine—and clearing Belleau Wood. As the General and I drove through these areas, we reminisced about the history we had read of the battles fought here, the conditions and the lives lost. We hit here in warm sunny weather. We were victors on the move. This contrasted with the mud and trenches of WW I. General Palmer would have been 18 and in military school. I was not yet born. Both infantry divisions continued to follow motorized in the armored wake to reach march objectives. Rear guard action was the best the enemy could offer in the way of resistance, except in Villers Cotterets, where stronger opposition was encountered on 29 August and the spearhead reached positions just north of the Aisne River. On 30 August the drive continued in the direction of Sedan, the old German gateway into France. The 3rd Armored captured Laon and reached positions between that city and the Aisne. The cavalry continued to reconnoiter in front of the armor and on the right flank pushed patrols as far as Rozy-Sur-Serre. The following infantry met no opposition.

Piano wire did the job of decapitating the unwary Jeep occupant, especially at night. A length of 2 x 2-inch steel angle welded vertically to the front bumper and sharpened to cut this wire was our answer. The ping of a wire intended for your neck was a disconcerting sound on an otherwise quiet night as you made an evening run to another unit. Just when I had convinced myself that the enemy had decided to give up and run for home, the General's driver and I had our own personal encounter with this cute little trick. We laughed for days after as we caught one another instinctively feeling our necks.

Most Jeeps soon became quite heavily laden with a layer of sandbags on the floor to absorb the blast of the smaller mines—the larger mines would roll a sandbagged Jeep. Evidence of this found along the road in the morning was jarring and kept one on the alert.

From the outskirts of Sedan, the Corps drive to the northeast was changed to north with a 90-degree change in direction by the armor, an amazing move. This was to send the spearhead racing north into Belgium and Mons, where VII Corps was to reverse completely the victory the Germans had scored there in 1914, thus achieving the most decisive victory of the war to date, and almost destroying Von Kluge's army, which was striving to get back to Germany and man the defenses of the Siegfried Line.

VII

The South Belgium Campaign

The evening of 2 September found us just inside Belgium, bunked down in our bedrolls in the offices of an abandoned sugar beet factory. I recall that there was a great deal of glass and most of it intact. I was concerned about any possible explosions in the vicinity and the danger from this glass. This caused me not to sleep as well as I might have. All was quiet when about midnight there was a sound much like a chopper with its blades beating the air. (Though of course there weren't any at this time.) I rolled out and went outside to see what was up. There, lumbering across the sky, was our first buzz bomb. We had several that first night. At first, our thoughts were that the darned things were headed for London, but later we learned that they were destined for Antwerp and its harbor. Now and then a motor would cut out and you would hear a loud explosion. These were malfunctions and they landed harmlessly in some field. My thoughts were, "That could have been right here!"

We had been victims of many rumors about German secret weapons. I feel we sort of lived under a cloud on this subject. First the miniature tanks I mentioned on the beach, then came the "Screaming Mimis" (rockets set along the roadside and fired at night with hideous screaming sounds), and now the buzz bombs. What would be next?

By 31 August, the VII Corps was advancing eastward from Laon toward Sedan and the Ardennes Forest. The 3rd

Armored Division was spearheading the advance, followed closely by the 1st and 9th Infantry Divisions. The 4th Cavalry Group (reinforced) screened the right flank. During the morning, authority was granted for the Corps to move to the north and take Mons, Belgium. Orders were quickly issued to the divisions and the cavalry by radio and liaison airplanes, and the Corps reformed for the advance in the new direction. With a minimum of delay, the 3rd Armored Division, followed by the 1st Infantry Division, turned to the north. The 9th Infantry Division advanced northeast toward Chimay. The 4th Cavalry Group, screening the Corps' right flank, continued eastward and, unassisted, secured Maisieres. By this action the Corps was formed in three spearheads—one to the north, one to the northeast, and one to the east. There was no continuous front, but rather a series of disconnected small actions with troops of all echelons engaged with groups of retreating and unorganized enemy. Meanwhile, in northeastern France and western Belgium, the remnants of the German army under Von Kluge were attempting to fight a rear-guard action back to Germany in order to regroup and organize the defense of the Siegfried Line. Their planned axis of withdrawal was the line from Mons to Namur, but they were not aware of the sudden change in direction of advance of the now northbound columns of the VII Corps.

In the South Belgium campaign, 2 to 12 September, the VII Corps inflicted a decisive defeat on the enemy. These ten days witnessed the capture of 37,910 prisoners and the liberation of some 2,500 square miles of Belgium. The rapidity and surprises of the VII Corps advance so disrupted German preparations for the defense of the Siegfried Line on the Corps front that a penetration was achieved with a minimum loss in personnel and equipment.

On the morning of 2 September, the 9th Infantry Division on the right entered Belgium near the border village of La Forge Philippe. That same afternoon, the 3rd Armored Division on the left crossed the border between France and Belgium below Mons, followed by the First Infantry Division, which operated on the exposed flank of the Corps.

Driving north with all three combat commands, each operating in two columns, or task forces, the 3rd Armored Division reached Mons and, while waiting for supplies, organized roadblocks and other defenses. Meanwhile, the 1st Infantry Division pressed north on the left flank of the Corps against scattered enemy resistance, and the 9th Infantry Division started the swing east to secure crossings of Meuse River between Namur and Givet.

On 3 September, the 3rd Armored and 1st Infantry Divisions cut off elements of five enemy divisions on their routes of withdrawal. The three-day battle of Mons (3 to 5 September) that ensued proved to be one of the most decisive and spectacular of the entire European operation. The Corps infantry and armor, supported by fighter-bombers flying column cover, took a heavy toll of the retreating German army. Nearly all elements, including artillery and service units of the attacking divisions, engaged the enemy in close combat. So fast was the advance of the VII Corps and so numerous the enemy that even a section of the Corps headquarters, en route to reconnoiter for a new command post, killed or wounded over 100 enemy and captured some 700 prisoners.

The result was a decisive defeat for the Germans. In the Battle of Mons the remnants of twenty German divisions were decimated. Fields and woods in the Maubeuge-Mons-Binche-Bavai area were filled with dead and wounded, while the roads were strewn with burned and abandoned guns, armored vehicles, and motor transports. Approximately 5,000 Germans were killed, more were wounded, and over 27,000 were taken prisoner.

We had driven down a road just inside Belgium through the first village three hours earlier, looking for a likely command post site. Finding none, we returned to the main road into Mons, in front of a massive German column headed for the Siegfried line. We didn't know this, of course. We met forward elements of the 3rd Armored Division moving into position and, though they didn't know it, into a confrontation and decisive battle.

Probably one of the greatest surprises of the early days of the conflict was the discovery that the Germans relied so heavily on horse-drawn equipment. Now here in the great battle south of Mons, the carnage included a large number of horses. Their task was to pull the supply wagons packed with food, clothing, and ammunition. In addition to that were the first-aid facilities, administrative records, and office equipment, which spilled out of them as the wagons were hit and destroyed. It was a pitiful sight to see these innocent animals caught in the carnage for which they had no responsibility.

On this date (5 September) the British Guards Armored Division took Brussels, Belgium, and our 1st Army advanced to the border of Luxembourg. In addition to the 32,000 enemy killed or captured by the VI Corps, 80,000 surrendered in southwestern France, including 20,000 to a single platoon of the U.S. 83rd Thunderfoot Division. We heard about this event. It included arranging for a flight of sixteen P47 fighter bombers to overfly the site of the surrender negotiation meeting. The ability of the junior officer to call up such potentially devastating firepower on his command so impressed the unit commander that he negotiated surrender on the spot. The Germans quit because they feared the murderous firepower of

American fighter bombers.

The Belgian people were different from the French and put forth an effort to be different. It started with their architecture, which seemed to be different when we looked at their homes. Their attitude was also different. As we traversed France and battled the Germans, the French waited for us to clean the debris of battle. The Belgiques went to work on it right away. In many cases they repaired bridges the Germans had blown before our engineers could get at them. I never saw the French do this. I had experiences only a few weeks apart in France where the FFI (free French) approached our jeep and told us of several Germans hiding in a building and asked that we go after them. We were three lightly armed Americans; they were half a dozen well-armed FFI. Later we encountered a group of Belgians who stopped us and asked for ammunition and grenades. They told us of part of a German company hiding nearby. They didn't want us to go after them. They just wanted grenades and ammunition. They would do the job. I had the distinct feeling that many of these Germans never saw a PW cage. Later, I heard that the Belgian mines enjoyed a significant increase in cheap labor at this point. The Belgians took great offense at the treatment the Germans had given them.

The 3rd Armored Division was relieved by the 1st Infantry Division of its position in the vicinity of Mons. On 5 September, while the 1st Infantry Division continued to engage the enemy east of the Bavai area, smashing a counterattack, the Corps directed its main effort eastward with the mission of crossing the Meuse River and seizing all existing bridges. Again the 3rd Armored Division was the spearhead. Moving in multiple columns, it drove through scattered enemy opposition to the important industrial center of Charleroi, where it reduced enemy resistance and liberated the city. The armor continued against moderate opposition to Namur. One combat command assaulted the city from the west. The other combat command secured the high ground to the northeast, invested the northern part of Namur, and before midnight of 5 September, seized bridge sites for crossing of the Sambre River.

Meanwhile, the 9th Infantry Division and the 4th Cavalry Group on the right flank of the Corps had moved east to the Meuse River, preparatory to making the difficult crossing. Cavalry reconnaissance revealed blown bridges and a well-fortified east bank, where the enemy had organized a determined resistance. At 0100 hours of 5 September, the 9th Infantry Division began its crossing of the Meuse River north of Givet, between Heer and Blaimont. In the face of heavy enemy fire, several battalions succeeded in crossing the river in assault boats and establishing a bridgehead. A number of the boats were sunk, others were forced to turn back, and casualties were high.

The General continued to reconnoiter up front in an effort to determine more effective ways of employing our artillery. Here in early September, with the countryside looking so great, it seemed a shame to be involved in such a deadly game. I determined that if all went well, I would come back some day to visit these friendly people and see this country while standing up. Just when I got such a thought in my mind, the enemy would take it out with some rounds of artillery too close for comfort and we would head for the ditch or the shelter of the friendly side of the tank. On most occasions the Kraut artillery didn't last long, and if you survived the first few rounds, you were OK. Knowing this was of only minor comfort when the earth around you was erupting. The sight of dead and wounded friendly troops being pulled back to some makeshift shelter is morale-shattering. I always felt that these sights would be more tolerable if I were allowed to pick up a weapon and fire back, but such was not my job. It was most frustrating.

On 6 September the 9th Infantry Division continued to expand its bridgehead across the Meuse against well-organized and determined enemy resistance. The "Der Fuehrer" Regiment of the 2nd SS "Das Reich" Panzer Division fought fanatically to hold Blaimont. Note that our troops fought "valiantly"; the enemy fought "fanatically." By evening, additional troops were landed south of the town, and the defenders were finally forced to evacuate, but not before they had made a desperate tank-infantry counterattack. Other elements of the division, supported by an armored task force from the 3rd Armored Division, attacked north toward Dinant against continuous resistance.

Our bomb disposal squads became adept at mine and bomb work, including such touchy tasks as assisting surgeons in the removal of a small, live explosive shell from a wounded soldier. The leader of our Bomb Disposal unit risked his life and that of the field hospital surgeon when they isolated the soldier in an abandoned house and spent ten hours removing a high explosive shell in a bloody all-night operation. The patient survived.

After bridges over the Sambre River were completed, the 3rd Armored Division eliminated enemy resistance in Namur and crossed the Meuse River. Utilizing routes on both sides of the Meuse, the armor advanced to Huy, where it seized additional bridgeheads. This action was opposed by small arms, antitank, and artillery fire. Meanwhile, with the mopping up at Mons completed, the 1st Infantry Division advanced in the zone of the 3rd Armored Division to Charleroi.

Continuing northeastward along the Meuse on 7 September, armored spearheads reached Liège, while to the south, infantry strengthened bridgeheads from Givet to Dinan against heavy opposition. Elements of the 1st Infantry Division reached Huy and relieved armored units holding the Meuse River bridgehead. The 4th Cavalry Group crossed the Meuse and continued to screen the right flank of the 9th Infantry Division. Enemy strong points to the east of the river consisted of infantry, generally in platoon to company strength, defending roadblocks supported by flanking machine gun fire. The 9th Infantry Division steadily advanced against increased resistance and difficult terrain. Armored columns met only scattered enemy opposition in the advance toward Liège, although heavy antitank and artillery fire were encountered. Mopping up of enemy stragglers from Mons and the wooded area along the Sambre River brought the total prisoners to 30,000.

The occupation of Liège was completed the following day. During 8 September, enemy resistance north of the Meuse River between Namur and Liège ceased except for a few remaining stragglers. South of the river, the enemy attempted to establish a defensive line that ran generally from Scheit to Tinlot to Modave to Heure. However, several penetrations forced the enemy to abandon this line and to attempt a delaying action by well-fortified roadblocks and communication centers.

An amusing story was told by the Red Cross Club Mobile girls about one of their number who responded to a certain general's comments that he was glad they were doing such a great job with the troops, but he hadn't seen a doughnut since he left England. The young lady decided to remedy that situation. She selected half a dozen of the Club Mobile's finest to present to the general. She then decided to sugar them, and had to search for sugar that had not become hard from moisture. Finally, she found a container that looked OK. She rolled the doughnuts, and sent them to the general. The next morning brought a call from the general's aide. Expecting a thank you or a request for more, she was surprised to hear that the general took one bite for his breakfast and uttered a few choice words, wondering what the heck these girls were serving to the troops. She had mistaken the salt for the sugar and had rolled the doughnuts in salt. So much for good impressions!

The 3rd Armored Division encountered determined enemy resistance at critical terrain features as it continued to advance the next day toward Verviers. South of the Vesdre River, on the right flank of the Corps zone, the 9th Infantry Division met stiffer resistance than the previous day. Most bridges were blown and covered by 20mm and antitank guns, while numerous roadblocks also slowed progress. While no definite enemy front line existed, we encountered strong points in villages along the way, and these were stubbornly held. At Louveigne, our troops encountered dug-in tanks, infantry, and artillery. Several ME-109 aircraft were active in the Corps zone of action.

As we approached the Belgian town of Verviers, we encountered a sad little procession. Six older gentlemen, dressed in black, carrying a casket. Family and friends followed this little procession, which was led by a clergyman. I was pleasantly surprised when General Palmer told the driver to pull over and stop. He just said, "All right, men, c'mon, this is the least we can do. Let's pay our respects." We followed his lead and stood at attention along the road by our Jeep, then saluted as the procession passed. I really hadn't thought the General was all that sensitive. The poor Belgians had been left with no vehicle to act as a hearse.

Positions in the vicinity of Verviers were consolidated on 10 September. The Corps prepared to drive into Germany, and the first artillery fire landed on German soil at 1723 hours.

On 11 September, troops of the Corps occupied Eupen, Malmédy, Stavelot, and Spa, and concentrated on the prewar German border in preparation for the attack on the Siegfried Line. The enemy attempted to resist the advance with active defense tactics, mounting a small-scale counterattack near Eupen. He employed long-range artillery, but his activity was largely confined to a screening action based on roadblocks and supported by minefields, antitank, and artillery fire.

On 12 September, as part of the VII Corps reconnaissance in force, elements of the 3rd Armored Division entered Germany. The Battle of South Belgium thus drew to a close, and the penetration of the Siegfried Line commenced.

In this short period of time, the VII Corps successfully completed a separate campaign involving difficult maneuvers and sustained drive, where speed was of the essence. While maintaining pressure in the original direction of movement, the Corps executed a 90-degree change in direction in one day. It cut off a German corps from withdrawal and annihilated it. It effected an opposed river crossing in the face of difficult terrain and continued to advance on a broad front without delay or rest for the troops. The rapid seizure of the crossings of the Meuse from Namur to Liège capitalized on the victory of Mons. In a total of ten days, the enemy had been driven from south Belgium.

Once again, American troops and commanders succeeded in battle because of their ability to make on-the-spot decisions and take the initiative. Throughout the ETO campaign, VII Corps put its faith in speed of movement rather than complicated coded messages. By the time the enemy got any of VII Corps' messages on where we were, and figured out counteraction, it was incumbent upon us to be gone! That was motivating force enough for us.

I had come away from my earlier experience with the 502nd jump battalion carrying an unwanted souvenir—one that I have kept the rest of my life. I had volunteered to jump in behind enemy lines on D-Day with a radio team to adjust or conduct fire from our Navy ships standing offshore. My fourth training jump in England was a "bummer." My stick of nine men caught a freak ground wind and I was one of several injured. I was knocked out and had my back jammed up, thus disqualifying me from my fifth and qualifying jump the next day. I was fortunate. Others had broken bones. I was deeply disappointed, but it may have saved my life in the long run. The problem was that this injury returned to plague me, and riding in the back of the Jeep or standing in the armored scout car for extended periods of time brought about great pain. General Palmer was very understanding of this as he had watched me struggle with the problem for weeks. He offered me the opportunity to pick another assignment if I wished. We agreed on my being assigned to the Corps Liaison Section, which allowed me a more comfortable ride in the front of my own Jeep. It worked. It was less prestigious, but better for my health. So, in mid-September, I became a combat liaison officer.

This was only the beginning of a long friendship with General Palmer, which lasted throughout the campaign. My association with him and identification with him was a tremendous help to me in the performance of my duties both as liaison officer and later on as public relations officer. When we encountered one another in the field, either inspecting some unit or just meeting on the road, he always inquired about my health and my work. He opened several doors for me as time went on. We were in contact by letter throughout the Korean War, in which he served as a Corps commander. I lunched with him in Washington on occasion, years later. At that time, he wore four stars and was Assistant Chief of Staff—G4. He was pleased that I had stayed in the reserves, and we philosophized about many aspects of our armed forces as years went by. In combat he was tough and demanding, but very effective.

So now, in mid-September, I became a liaison officer in Corps headquarters. My task, along with that of several other officers, was to make contact with divisions or other units as assigned by Corps G-2 (Intelligence). I was then to determine the exact position of their forward elements, determine the progress they were making, the nature of the resistance they were encountering, and any other intelligence I could glean, then take it all back to Corps in a timely fashion. At times I bunked down with my assigned unit for a few days and advised Corps by coded phone message. At other times I called for a liaison plane and flew my information back. At other times, I commuted by Jeep. It all depended on the circumstances—enemy action, weather, urgency of the information at hand.

As battles heated up, I would catch the spirit of the game and work for long hours to gather intelligence and get it back to Corps. I always aimed to be first to get the latest. I figured I could sleep some other day. War is really for the young and idealistic!

It was pretty much left up to me to determine the quality and urgency of the information I had gathered. This was a position I enjoyed, even though it was rougher and more demanding at times. It required more personal initiative.

Our POW count was now mounting to a total of 50,700 for this particular action, or 111,000 from D-Day to now. POWs by the truckload were passing down the roads every day. Our holding pens became crowded and facilities were strained. It was not too unusual to meet a handful of GIs in Jeeps escorting hundreds of docile POWs to the rear.

The worst single day's disaster other than Omaha Beach landing losses. Over 700 troops and all their tanks and equipment slid into the sea from this and other LSTs. This one made it back to the harbor at Dartmouth.

Our jump master, Corporal Cheney, took this picture for me with my camera as I landed on my first jump. He came over to me as I landed, looked down at me, and said with disappointment, "Landed like a feather. I knew you would!" That was great, but the fourth jump was another story.

LCI (Landing Craft Infantry) headed for Utah Beach: D-Day.

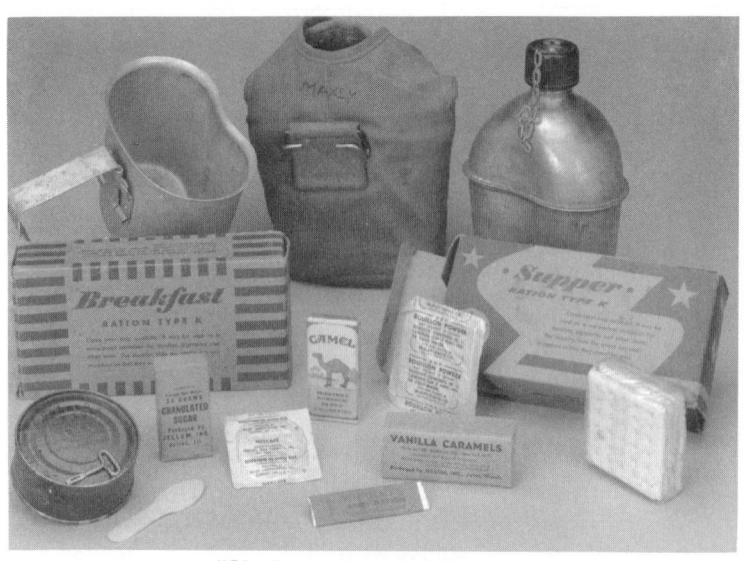

"Sir! Dinner is served!"

"Alles kaput!" My souvenir P-38 pistol.

Normandy - Utah Beach. D+6. Note relaxed atmosphere. Men congregating, telephone wire reel in right foreground, tractor - towed 155 mm howitzers at mid and right as well as 155 mm "Long Tom" on road in front of mobile cranes. Engineer's bull dozer prepares hard stand for supply stockpiling at left. Beached L.C.I.s and L.S.T.s farther out with protective barage balloons

© MICHELIN from Map No. 102, No. 409. Permission No. 9612621.

About half of the class of twenty-five field artillery officers who volunteered for the D-Day jump. I took this picture when we arrived for training. My friend Lt. Bob Evans from the 951st is at lower left with the cigarette.

The mission of the Sherman tank was, from time to time, just to provide a mobile shield from snipers for the infantry as we inched our way through a town. This meant that only three flanks had to be covered.

This British glider didn't quite make it through the hedge row. An American General aboard was killed in this action.

This re-enactment on D-Day plus 50 years of the paratrooper hanging from the St.MereEglise church steeple brought back memories.. I saw the empty parachute on D +3.

© MICHELIN from Map No. 102, No. 409. Permission No. 9612621.

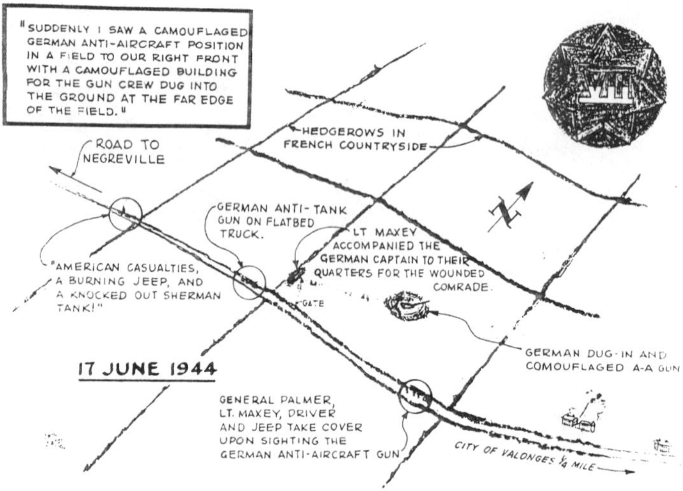
"SUDDENLY I SAW A CAMOUFLAGED GERMAN ANTI-AIRCRAFT POSITION IN A FIELD TO OUR RIGHT FRONT WITH A CAMOUFLAGED BUILDING FOR THE GUN CREW DUG INTO THE GROUND AT THE FAR EDGE OF THE FIELD."
HEDGEROWS IN FRENCH COUNTRYSIDE
ROAD TO NEGREVILLE
GERMAN ANTI-TANK GUN ON FLATBED TRUCK.
LT MAXEY ACCOMPANIED THE GERMAN CAPTAIN TO THEIR QUARTERS FOR THE WOUNDED COMRADE.
"AMERICAN CASUALTIES, A BURNING JEEP, AND A KNOCKED OUT SHERMAN TANK!"
GATE
GERMAN DUG-IN AND COMOUFLAGED A-A GUN
17 JUNE 1944
GENERAL PALMER, LT. MAXEY, DRIVER AND JEEP TAKE COVER UPON SIGHTING THE GERMAN ANTI-AIRCRAFT GUN
CITY OF VALONGES 1/4 MILE

Armored scout car and crew
(I am in the center) as well as the Tommy gun were
all added equipment after the incident described below.

Anti-Aircraft gun emplacement on the Valognes/Negreville road.
This was the site of the capture of 21 officers and men by Brig. Gen.
Williston Palmer, Lt. Wm. Maxey and their driver. June 17, 1944.

© MICHELIN from Map No. 102, No. 409. Permission No. 9612621.

Normandy, June 25, 1944.
Our artillery fired blind at elevation zero through the hedges. Scene shows enemy tanks "still cooking".
Lower right - ammo starts exploding again as I try for a close-up. This was the source
of my P-38 pistol souvenir.. See last photo in book.

© MICHELIN from Map No. 102, No. 409. Permission No. 9612621.

The eight-inch howitzer on the march towed by a full-track prime mover. The drivers of this equipment were highly skilled.

The M-7 howitzer motor carriage known as the Priest. Note the ringmount on the right front equipped with a .50-caliber machine gun. Many of the two-and-a-half-ton trucks were so equipped as antiaircraft protection.

Goliath, the German remote-controlled minitank as found on the beach when we arrived. These tanks carried a reel with nine-tenths of a mile of three-strand wire—two strands for guiding and one strand for detonating the 132-pound explosive charge carried aboard.

Clockwise

1. Lt. Jack Wedon inspects Siegfried Line pill box. It had been a "cottage" until our tank blew off the fake roof.

2. Siegfried Line dragon's teeth viewed from top of pill box.

3. Maxey passes through the line of tank traps.

© MICHELIN from Map No. 102, No. 409. Permission No. 9612621.

This small hotel was our liaison office until the front shifted and we chose to vacate while the going was good. The building was OK when we arrived (but the food service was never too good). The enemy decided to improve the ventilation and it looked like this when I visited this town a few days later.

This was the back side of the bank in Aachen which took another of those 16" shells while I departed on the other side. It seems the Germans were poor losers, at times. This almost cost me a good pair of Ray-Ban sun glasses!

© MICHELIN from Map No. 102, No. 409. Permission No. 9612621.

Generals Eisenhower, Bradley, Hodges and Collins at Kur Hotel, Petersburg, Germany. March 26, 1945.

Major General J. Lawton Collins, VII Corps Commander and Brigadier General Williston B. Palmer at Kur Hotel with the Rhine River Valley in the background. March 26, 1945.

© MICHELIN from Map No. 102, No. 409. Permission No. 9612621.

Generals Bradley, Allen and Eisenhower at 104th Division Headquarters in the field.

Field Marshal Montgomery visits Gen. Terry Allen of "Timber Wolf" fame at Division Hqrs in the field

"MONTY"   ALLEN

© MICHELIN from Map No. 102, No. 409. Permission No. 9612621.

Clockwise

1. The enemy destroyed bridges as they retreated in a futile attempt to halt our advance.
2. The castle in Stolberg looks down on a strange sight - enemy soldiers.
3. An unmanned German 88mm gun guards an autobahn intersection.
4. German armored personnel carrier.
5. Truck-mounted 88mm gun took a hit from our artillery.

© MICHELIN from Map No. 102, No. 409. Permission No. 9612621.

© MICHELIN from Map No. 102, No. 409. Permission No. 9612621.

Site of 2nd slave labor camp at Nordhausen, Germany, April 1945. This is the entrance to the V-1/V-2 bomb plant consisting of miles of tunnels dug by slave laborers. Most died of respiratory diseases. Camp had a "hospital" where patients died in bunk beds. Eight patients were still alive when I got there and I met one again on a construction job in Chicago area in 1969.

© MICHELIN from Map No. 102, No. 409. Permission No. 9612621.

Slave labor factory ,Nordhausen, parking lot. Photo No.2.

© MICHELIN from Map No. 102, No. 409. Permission No. 9612621.

The Germans really didn't want us to use their bridges. These were over the Meuse River in Belgium.

© MICHELIN from Map No. 102, No. 409. Permission No. 9612621.

The devastated city of Duren, Germany. Both the German citizens and our Corps of Engineers did a quick job of cleaning the streets of the debris of battle. After months of bombing and shelling everyone was anxious to get on the road to as much normalcy as possible.

The pillbox at the edge of town was destroyed by our engineers. In the event of a sneek counter-attack, we didn't want it to be recycled.

© MICHELIN from Map No. 102, No. 409. Permission No. 9612621.

Date : Sept. 12, 1944

The battle of Mons, Belgium. Vast amounts of materiel were destroyed in this 10 day battle. Over 31,900 soldiers were captured and thousands were killed in this action. A complete reversal of the WW I Allied defeat here. This prevented their intended occupation of the Seigfried Line.

"Set some extra places for dinner tonight, Sergeant, we have company".

© MICHELIN from Map No. 102, No. 409. Permission No. 9612621.

American Waco glider bringing in supplies D+2/D+3. Note identifying white stripes on all Allied aircraft.

Here in Bonn on the Rhine my first Public Relations Office (PRO) set up as promised. Furnished to the hilt and ready to receive all dignitaries. My driver found this super-sized champagne bottle to be cardboard and very dry.

The Leipzig Fire Insurance Building hosted the last VII Corps Hqrs. in Germany. (Jayhawk) Pictured beside my PRO signe is Pfc. Mason Fry, a High School classmate whom I found in one of our subordinate units and had brought up to Corps for a couple of days of reunion. May, 1945

© MICHELIN from Map No. 102, No. 409. Permission No. 9612621.

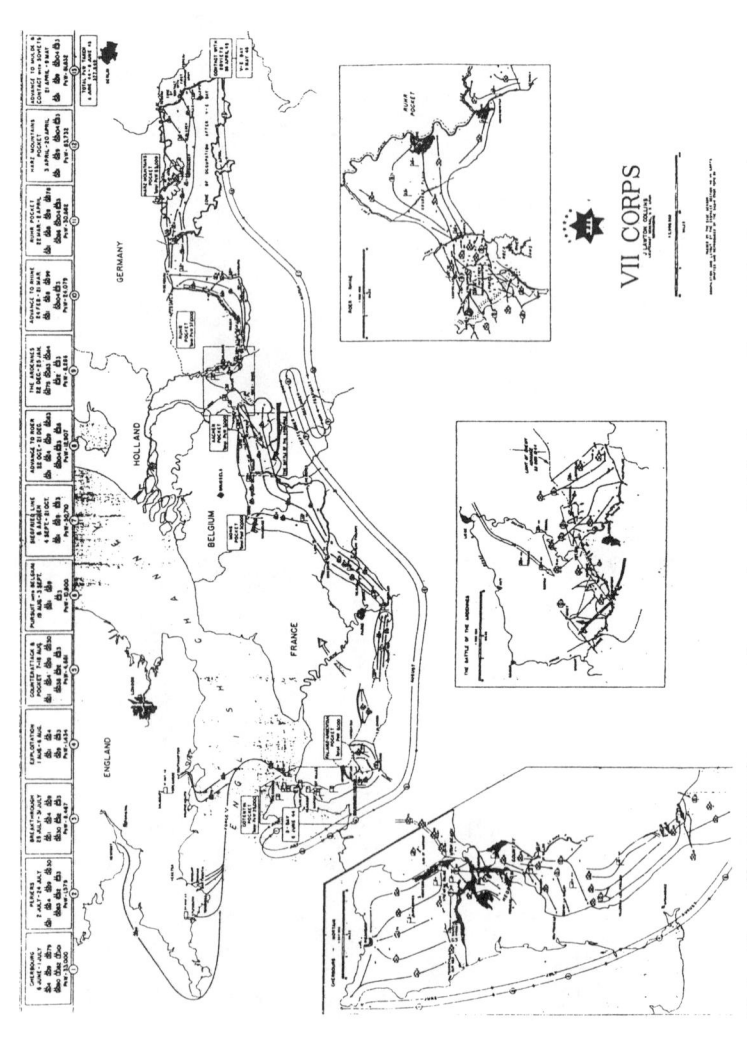

Note: Complimentary larger-scale map is available from author, 1100 Pembridge Drive, Apt. 315, Lake Forest, IL 60045

Map Notes:

The map accompanying this narrative is a serious and important part of the effort to tell the story. If the reader will take a few moments to become acquainted with its attributes he can identify the locale of any of the points of interest discussed herein.

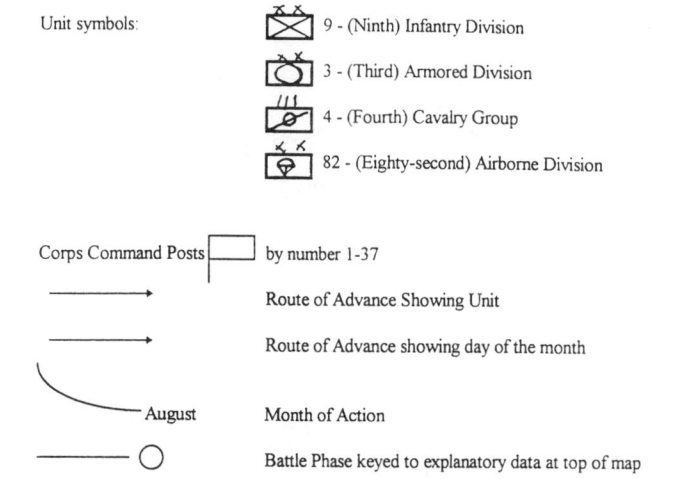

Unit symbols:

9 - (Ninth) Infantry Division

3 - (Third) Armored Division

4 - (Fourth) Cavalry Group

82 - (Eighty-second) Airborne Division

Corps Command Posts — by number 1-37

Route of Advance Showing Unit

Route of Advance showing day of the month

August — Month of Action

Battle Phase keyed to explanatory data at top of map

Capt. Wm. Carson Rogers- Life saver.

The sixteen inch RR gun shells intended for VII Corps Headquarters buildings at Kornelimunster were fired from 20 miles away and missed by less than 50 yards, but scored these hits.

Upper left

My quarters for a week till the night before when Capt Wm.Carson Rogers convinced me to move up the valley road and join him and others in a house they had comandeered. He saved my neck!

Guard tower at the corner of our coumpound took a near miss. The second floor , a circular wooden platform , went up a couple of feet and then floated down with two off--duty guards in their sleeping bags.

© MICHELIN from Map No. 102, No. 409. Permission No. 9612621.

VIII

The Push to the Roer River

By D + 100 days the Corps had hurled the "Blitzkrieg" back to the land of its origin. The spearhead of the First U.S. Army crossed the German border on 12 September and three days later completely pierced Hitler's vaunted Siegfried Line. It was the first invasion of Germany in force since Napoleon.

To the Corps' own spearhead 3rd Armored Division went the honor of being the first unit to enter Germany. At 1451 hours on 12 September, this great division passed the last frontier east of Eupen. A few minutes later elements of the First Division entered Germany proper in the vicinity of Aachen. On this day, elements of the Corps were deployed in Germany, Holland, and Belgium, with rear echelons in France. And of greater importance, I was saying to myself, "One year ago on this date you and Eva Vincent were walking down the church aisle back in Polo, Illinois, getting married." What a difference a year makes. I found both events reason to celebrate, but lacked the time and means. I wanted desperately to write to Eva and relate the details of this day, but censorship restricted what I could say. We knew the war was not yet over, but this *had* to be a benchmark and one step closer to home.

Our anticipation of the great difficulties in breaching the Siegfried Line proved to be exaggerated because of the success in cutting off the German forces in Belgium. As I drove around the first dragon's teeth and viewed the miles of pyramidal concrete obstacles to my right and left, I could visualize the murderous task of getting through them if they'd been covered by enemy machine guns and 88s. In some areas this cover was there, but in others—such as where I came through—it was not. In many locations there were obvious heavy concrete bunkers with ominous gun ports. In others there were small cottages placed in the landscape with windows and pitched roofs. They looked so innocent. A few well-placed rounds from a tank to my front changed the scene. The roofs exploded off and a concrete bunker was revealed. The windows were just black indentations, some with curtains that had been painted on them. The front door concealed a gun port. The greatest weakness of the entire line was the lack of manpower to back it up. Some bunkers were not manned.

> "The sacred soil of Germany shall never be invaded by the enemies of the Reich."
> —Adolf Hitler.

It was not until the next day that the 9th Division crossed the old pre-war border of Germany, south of Rotgen. This same day, Rotgen itself became the first German town to fall to the Allies in the west when it was captured by the Reconnaissance Battalion of the 3rd Armored Division. Other elements of "The Spearhead" made the first breach of the Siegfried Line in the vicinity of Scheidmuchle.

On 14 September, the 47th Infantry advanced through the Siegfried Line, penetrating both the first and second zone of defenses while the other two regiments of the 9th Division drove into the Hurtgen Forest.

Life in combat yields a little chuckle every now and then, even when things are rough. My driver (and I had several as time passed) on one particular occasion as we moved from Belgium into Germany was a nervous type. As we drove along with a row of low hills off to our left, I could see he was struggling with himself and sort of stroking the steering wheel nervously. As we kept hearing a series of explosions just beyond the ridge on our left and I'm thinking *I hope they don't shift a few hundred yards our way or our goose will be cooked!*, my driver said, "I'm sure glad those are all going out!" I replied, "Me too, John. Me too." We didn't have any artillery for five miles around! No harm done, John calmed down, and I got a big laugh to myself. What you don't know *can* hurt you, but no sense crying until it does.

By 15 September, Combat Command Hickey of the 3rd Armored Division had completely pierced the Siegfried Line's dragon's teeth, pillboxes, and antitank defenses. This formidable defensive barrier also was breached entirely by the 1st Division on the 15th. The Corps was ready for further exploitation and pursuit of the disorganized enemy. However, supplies had failed to keep pace with the rapid movement of our troops, and higher headquarters directed that we stop. I recall the frustration expressed by General Collins at staff meetings. We had the enemy on the run. The division commanders were eager to go. You could hear it in their voices, and yet we could not move because of the supply situation. The GIs in the trucks and tanks were all second-guessing the "brass" and bitching about being ordered to halt and dig in. The Corps was limited to small attacks, but on 22 September Stolberg became the first German city to fall when tank-infantry elements completed mopping-up operations. For the first time in centuries, the castle on the hill overlooking the main street in town witnessed a triumphant enemy force. The ghosts in that dour old edifice must have spent a sleepless night.

An interesting little monument developed on a man-made knoll near Eilendorf. A P-47 returning from its mission had been gunned down, but was almost intact. He came down in a field wheels-up and skidded on his belly for some distance, coming to a halt on top of a knoll. Amusingly enough, this "knoll" was a part of the Siegfried Line—a bunker with soil in the back but concrete in front. The plane looked intact and a bit incredible as we arrived. We could see it in the distance. The pilot escaped to our lines and told me he would have had an immediate nervous breakdown if he had been aware of the fact that a German bunker was right under his floorboards. Our troops took the bunker before the day was out and only put a few holes in the P-47.

Troops must have their fun from time to time. One such occasion occurred in Aachen. We were stalled for lack of fuel in our vehicles because Patton's army had usurped our supplies. The enemy had let up on its attacks. An interurban train had operated between Aachen and towns to the east, and, of course, was no longer being used. On a small hill in Aachen, our soldiers found a lone rail car in good shape. They loaded it with fused shells, land mines, and other explosives. A long fuse was attached and at night a truck was brought up to push the car. As it gained momentum, a soldier lit the fuse and jumped off. It glided quietly through the night across our lines and, at about 2:00 A.M., into the enemy lines. By this time the enemy was firing at it without realizing what it was. It exploded, leaving a crater we later had to fill, and probably few, if any, enemy casualties, but a big laugh for our troops and an evening of entertainment.

In mid-September, the Corps command post was

moved to the small valley town of Kornielimunster, south of Aachen. We occupied a plethora of buildings which I assumed had at one time been a Catholic school or convent and more recently a Nazi headquarters of some sort, according to the trappings left around. The buildings were situated around a large cobblestone courtyard. At one corner of the yard, some distance from the larger buildings, was a three-story guard tower constructed of fieldstone. Across the yard was a two-story school building. At this particular time, I had office duty in the liaison map room. I had selected a school classroom as a good spot to roll out my bedroll. After a few weeks there, Capt. Carson Rogers, Liaison Officer from one of our support units, suggested that I join him and some others in a house they had taken over up the valley road about a quarter of a mile from the main complex. It seemed like a good idea and far less lonesome than my present quarters. By this time, nearby resistance had been cleared out and Aachen had been captured. Almost immediately, I was to be made aware of what a great idea this move was. The night after I accepted this kind invitation, we heard the familiar sound of an artillery shell coming through the air. By now we could pretty well identify the size of shells by the sound they made. This was a big one. It sounded like a shell from a naval gun, possibly a 16-incher. This far inland, the only answer was a railroad gun. It sounded like a boxcar.

The first round landed on a ridge above our complex, shattering the night. It killed a sentry and a major who had stopped to ask directions. The second round took out the base of the stone guard tower and rolled the tank occupied by the "palace guard" at the corner of the courtyard. The third round took out the back of my recently vacated school building, and made that heavy masonry building look like Swiss cheese. Thank you, Captain Rogers—you saved my life! The fourth landed up the valley in some abandoned buildings.

Inspection the next morning and analysis of the attack made it clear that the complex housing Corps headquarters was the intended target. At a range of probably thirty miles or so, only a slight error in setting the gun had resulted in a fifty-yard change in deflection, and salvation for our headquarters. The range had been perfectly calculated. Now the question was, what pitiful little old lady had managed to talk her way through our lines and inform the enemy as to the location of this Corps headquarters?

The American Red Cross doughnut girls (including the crews of the Bearcat, the Buckeye, and the Magnolia) happened to be quartered at Corps headquarters this night with some of their trucks. It was a night of terror for them. This was, however, not all that novel. These girls were in harm's way all too frequently, but still continued to hand out that most welcome "spud" and a hot cup of "java" (as well as a genuine American-girl smile).

Later, in Aachen, while visiting the regimental headquarters of one of the 104th Division's units, I was to experience another visit from this gun when it wiped out the regimental command post, situated in a bank building, killing numerous people—and only moments after my visit, while I was crossing the street to use a phone set up in what was left of a small tavern. I think those Krauts were trying to tell me something. I was showered with bits and pieces of masonry and mortar and plaster dust. I was knocked to my knees by the concussion. The only real damage was a lungful of dust for a while and the loss of my prized Ray-Ban sunglasses. They wound up with bent frames and a broken lens. All this and still no Purple Heart! Coincidentally, I had been reading a magazine sent from home that carried an ad for this brand of glasses, including the company address. In a day or so I relocated the ad, packaged up the glasses, and sent them off to the company with instructions to send the repair bill to my wife, Eva, in Green Bay, Wisconsin. Much to my surprise, a few weeks later a package arrived with my repaired sunglasses and a note that read, "No Charge. Good luck, soldier." By golly, it made a guy feel this was all worthwhile.

Seeing and hearing the huge flights of B-17s flying over en route to their targets in the heart of Germany was a delight. Antiaircraft fire at the front was minor because the enemy didn't have many guns up front capable of reaching those high-flying planes. After a time, the bombers were due to return and we would try to count the planes in each formation and watch for those in trouble. From time to time parachutes would blossom and we would have "guests." It always bothered me to see how many of these crew members injured themselves on landing. They told me they didn't really train for jumps. They just assumed they wouldn't need to.

One evening as I was returning to our headquarters and a flight was returning high overhead, I became aware of an increase in the German ack-ack fire up front. I stopped to see what kind of targets the Germans had found. Coming in at less than 2,000 feet was one of our B-17s. One motor was out. The rest were functioning, though throttled back. The plane was flying in a wide, lazy arc, finally crossing over into friendly territory, and the firing ceased. It continued on in its arc behind me and finally returned to enemy territory some distance from me. I could hear the German ack-ack pick up again as it returned to enemy territory. That was a sad evening, as I contemplated that gallant ship having taken so much punishment and still returning. How long did it last? What was the fate of its crew? Why was it put on automatic pilot and abandoned? Were injured or dead still on board? It gave me the creeps to contemplate the answers to these questions. The official report would be "one of our planes is missing"—there was much, much more to that story, and I guess no one will ever know it.

From time to time, German trains were caught en route to the homeland and our Air Force cut their trip short. Our troops had a field day! Furs and silks from Paris plus wines, champagnes, liqueurs, and whiskey, as well as other treasures were spilled out of the cars. I expect some of the finery made it back to France as barter and made the girls very happy there. A friend supplied me with a case of champagne, which I carried under a canvas tarp in the back of my Jeep till it "evaporated" a little more each night. Still don't care for the stuff.

During the next two months, the only VII Corps offensive operation that attracted attention from other than military experts was the encirclement and capture of Aachen. October 5th was an unusual day and night for our Corps and its antiaircraft units. The Luftwaffe made a show of muscle. All day and all night they bombed and strafed in the Corps area near Aachen. They certainly caused damage, but not as much as our guys did. Out of the approximately seventy-five planes participating, our antiaircraft artillery and multiple-mount 50-caliber machine guns reported downing twenty-seven and seriously damaging twenty-four more. I had become acquainted with a young corporal from Peoria, Illinois, and he manned a multiple 50-caliber gun close to the house I occupied. He was so happy with his "kills," you would have thought he had won the war. He told me it was the first time in this "whole damned war" that he felt that he had earned his keep. This ancient city of Aachen, once the capitol of Charlemagne's Empire of the West, fell to the Corps on 21 October. It was the first major German city to be captured in the west.

Eva was quite an expert at packing and sending all sorts of items. I always looked forward to these packages for several reasons: I admired her thoughtfulness in picking items I could use and enjoy, of course, but her ability to pack items that nestled into a cube with no voids in the package was a work of art. All went well until she sent a block of chocolate fudge she had made and poured directly into a tea tin. She had sacrificed her sugar ration for this venture—sadly, as it turned out, because by the time it arrived the fudge shared the tin with the darndest batch of mold.

When our GIs are stuck for a brief time in one location, one can expect that they will busy themselves improving their situation. As time passes, this process continues. The foxhole becomes a mini-home if the situation permits. A seat is improvised—possibly a salvaged chair or car seat. A grenade sump is dug almost before a cover is improvised. If a grenade is tossed into our GI's home, he needs a hole for it to roll into. He may not be able to hear for weeks, but at least he will survive the grenade that explodes in that pit. A can of some sort for sand and fuel for cooking and heating is procured if the enemy is distant enough. Eventually, many items that the soldier has "liberated" along the way will decorate his hole in the ground. A sudden order to "move out" results in many foxhole treasures being left behind, although I was told of an amusing incident in the Hurtgen Forest. It seems one soldier had found a beautiful, highly polished table-model radio left in a demolished house. This Philips radio was too much of a prize to be left behind. As he advanced from tree to tree, he would lug this radio in one hand and his weapon in the other—put the radio down—fire off a few rounds—pick up the radio—and dash for the next cover. The teller of the story didn't know if the radio or the soldier survived the battle.

When the battered city of Aachen fell, the Germans lost more than a cultural and historic landmark, an important industrial center of the coal producing area, and a border fortress. Ancient Aachen (Aix-la-Chapelle), the Imperial City, was a symbol of heroic resistance for the Nazis, and its successful defense was to have been a symbol of the Reich's invulnerability. It had been ordered defended to the last man. On occasion, Hitler was very honest with his people. His prophecy that "give me five years and you will not recognize Germany again," was certainly carried out in Aachen. Our engineers liked the prophecy so well that they lettered up a large sign and placed it in one of the town squares. Wouldn't you know? No film in my camera that day! While Aachen was making the headlines, much hard fighting was in progress to the south, especially in the bloody Hurtgen Forest, where the veteran 9th Infantry Division again distinguished itself. After fighting its way through the forest, knocking out many pillboxes to reach the towns of Vossenack and Germeter, a series of determined counterattacks was stopped in spite of its long, thinly held line. Casualties of the 9th Division alone were more than 2,400 for October, and late September's were proportionately as high.

October 14th. The news of Rommel's suicide is met with mixed emotions in our headquarters. Certainly, it eliminated a formidable foe, but it would have been more honorable and fitting had this worthy enemy died in battle.

By mid-November the Corps was ordered to resume the attack and on the 16th it got underway. The 4th Division, back from its Paris assignment, had replaced the battered and weary 9th Division in the line in the Hurtgen Forest area, and the 3rd Armored and 1st Infantry Divisions continued to operate in the center and on the left flank of the Corps. But something new had been added; it was Major General Terry Allen's 104th Infantry Division. The Timberwolves were committed between the 4th Infantry and 3rd Armored Divisions. The Spearhead made rapid progress and captured the important objective of Werth and by the end of the second day had occupied all its objectives, including both Hasternath and Scherpenseel. The Red One, (1st) Division, with a Regimental Combat Team of the 9th Infantry attached, cleared Gressenich and were fighting in Hamich. In the Hurtgen Forest, the 4th Division found the going tough.

Resistance was much stiffer across the whole front than during September, when the Wehrmacht, weary and groggy from the battering and repeated defeats of the previous three months, was tottering on the verge of collapse. Now they were able to present a solid front. New units had come into the line and every village in the Eschweiler-Weisweiller area was turned into a fanatically defended strong point. At the same time, we had been forced to give them a rest because of our supply problems.

November 17, 1944. Fighting raged from the Netherlands to the Vosges mountains in France, with six Allied armies trying to break through to the Rhine.

A wild shoot-out erupted north of Aachen when the U.S. 2nd Hell on Wheels Armored division pulverized a counterattack by the Wehrmacht's 9th Panzer. Nearly every 2nd Armored vehicle, including the division's bulldozers, took part in the fight.

While the dependable 1st Division slowly pushed on from one objective to another against very determined opposition, the 4th Division made costly progress in the Hurtgen Forest, and on some days gains were measured in yards. It was now that the 104th Infantry Division, with its fresh blood, stepped out to pace the attack. In a brilliant series of night operations, the Timberwolves mopped up one town after another and during daylight of 22 November eliminated the last German resistance in Eschweiler. The attack persisted against stubborn opposition and enemy counterthrusts. On the right flank, elements advanced through the forest north and west of Gressnau, finally taking the town on the 29th. By this time, the 104th Division had advance elements in Lamersdorf and Inden, where strong enemy attacks were repulsed, and the 1st Division pushed through to Lamersdorf. November's fighting cost the Corps 10,000 casualties.

Gambling is just in the blood of some guys, and they are always trying to put a game together. We had one big lieutenant colonel who was in Corps headquarters and who was of this ilk. I never accepted his invitation and was glad I didn't as time went by. One winter night in Kornielimunster, the Colonel got a good game going and the cards were going his way. A potbellied cast iron stove stood in the corner of the room and the fire was going as good as the game. The Colonel had found a couple of bottles of "firewater" of some sort, which added to the spirit of the occasion. As the evening wore on, the Colonel's game went from one of those "can't lose" situations to "can't win." Nothing worked for him, and he borrowed what he could, then lost his temper. Finally, he totally lost his cool, stood up, doubled up his big fists and hit the potbellied stove, caving in its very hot side.

He lost his temper, the game, the bones in his right hand, his job at Corps headquarters, and his rank all at once. He was court-martialed within days and reassigned.

Obtaining accurate and current information to send or take into Corps headquarters should not be all that difficult for a liaison officer from another good headquarters. We were all on the same team. Nevertheless, at times regimental or even divisional staffs were reluctant to divulge locations of forward elements to a lieutenant. This, even though he claimed to represent higher headquarters. I was fortunate in this respect because I had met many of the top staff officers, including the general officers, while serving as General Palmer's aide. It opened doors for me and increased my effectiveness.

I encountered General Palmer driving through a village one day and he pulled over to inquire about how things were going. I told him that I was trying to get information from the headquarters of this new division in the vicinity where we were, but couldn't make the grade. I had no contact on the division staff. General Palmer scowled and said, "Goddammit, Bill, that's ridiculous. Get in your Jeep and follow me." Fifteen minutes later General Palmer, his aide, the Division Commanding General, his G-2 intelligence colonel, and I were having the friendliest chat on how he could help me expedite getting material back to the VII Corps. It paid to know the right person!

In late November, 1944, while on duty in the Corps Liaison Office, I was advised that the Army was contemplating the establishment of a super high-powered radio transmitter-receiver to be constructed in Belgium. It was to be capable of direct communication with London and Washington and was to be composed of several vans loaded with equipment as well as some very tall antenna masts. My immediate superior, Lieutenant Colonel Barnes, called me in and advised me that a staff of officers and enlisted men was being selected to man this facility. It would be composed mostly of communication experts but there would be some administrative persons, too. He told me this should be a desirable assignment with first-class quarters. He said he had put my name in for one of the administrative jobs and I had been accepted. I would hear more in a few weeks and be sent to some headquarters for training. It all sounded great and I thanked him. I could unpack my duffel, get my uniform cleaned, and live in a civilized manner for the rest of this war.

Well, Hitler had other plans. The Battle of the Bulge interrupted the radio project and my choice assignment. The need for the facility was reevaluated at the end of the Battle of the Bulge and it was dropped.

With December came more hard fighting, but the attack progressed and Lucherberg and Luchem were cleared. After a brief regrouping period, with the 9th Infantry Division replacing the 1st Division in the line while the latter moved back to a rest area, and with the 83rd Infantry Division progressively taking over from the battered 4th Division in the Hurtgen Forest, the attack was renewed.

Strass and Gey fell in very hard fighting, the 9th Division cleared Merode, and the 104th Division broke through the German defenses to the north to reach the Roer River, seizing Marken, Pier, and Schophoven. On 14 December all resistance within the 104th Infantry Division zone west of the Roer ended. The 9th Division also mopped up to the river line and these two divisions commenced patrolling along the stream while heavy fighting still continued on the right flank.

Elements of the 5th Armored Division were attached to the Corps, and in conjunction with units of the 83rd Infantry also succeeded in reaching the line of the Roer. By 18 December the Corps zone was cleared to the river.

Plans had been prepared for the attack across the Roer toward the important communication center of Eupen when the Germans launched their winter counteroffensive to the south of VII Corps. As the enemy penetration progressed, both the 1st and 9th Divisions were detached and moved south to meet the new threat, and finally the 3rd Armored Division followed. All this was the beginning of what was later to be known as the "Battle of the Bulge."

Monty was once more put in charge of all troops from the mid-point of the breakthrough north. This, at his request, brought General Collins and his VII Corps back under his command to the satisfaction of both, for they held each other in mutual respect. Both were aggressive, both believed in taking care of the troops, and both believed in being seen by their troops up front. Not only were Collins and Palmer seen up front, but they insisted on close-in support by their Field Artillery. Never did the troops complain that our artillery couldn't reach the targets in front of them. During this action, Monty toured the front in his Rolls-Royce, lifting the morale of the troops who saw him. He was notably successful at this throughout the campaign. He once drove into a Division headquarters in a neighboring Corps and found a disturbing atmosphere of near panic. He was told, "We are in grave danger; we have been cut off!" To which he replied, "That's funny, I just drove in here!"

On 18 December, 1944, two Panzer armies punched a

hole 50 miles wide from Malmédy to Echtenwach, Belgium, and up to twenty miles deep into our lines. Any hunter with wild game experience could have predicted this death-throes reaction from the wild beast called Adolf Hitler. While several American generals went into shock—including Ike and Hodges, according to Monty—Monty was unsurprised and accepted the whole thing as a magnificent challenge.

Monty believed in and used liaison officers to keep him informed on battlefield conditions. These officers and their function were an integral part of his headquarters. The American Unit Table of Organization did not even mention liaison officers, but added them informally in combat as the need became obvious. These officers were intended to keep their command informed of every possible detail of the situation up front, to the rear, and to each flank. General Palmer and I got out in front of our lead elements several times as a direct result of failure of our liaison section to keep our maps current in the early days of combat. This prompted my desire to join this office and add some more enthusiasm to its assigned task. There was no end to the useful information to be taken to Corps' headquarters from adjacent units, as well as subordinate units, if one just looked for it.

Meanwhile, Patton disengaged himself in the south and swung north with three divisions, attacking the Bulge from the south.

Now came time for the VII Corps to take a hand. Turning the Eupen area over to the XIX Corps along with the 104th Division, which staked the Corps' claim to the sector for future operations, VII Corps moved south on 22 December. The Corps' only participation so far in this fighting had been limited to mopping up parachutists whose airborne attack to seize the road center of Eupen behind our lines was foiled largely by our artillerymen. Antiaircraft gunners destroyed more than 100 enemy planes in several days as the Luftwaffe made its appearance in strength.

IX

The Belgian Bulge

To head off the rapid German winter offensive, VII Corps on 21 December was ordered to the Marche area, and after being relieved of its area along the Roer River moved to assembly areas southwest of Liège. The Corps had a front of 65 kilometers along the right flank of the First Army.

Late in the afternoon of the 21st, Lieutenant Colonel Barnes, head of the Corps liaison section, called me into his Kornielimunster office and showed me a map of the Bastogne-Marche, Belgium, area. It had been marked with wax pencil showing defensive positions for three divisions. He said I had been preceded earlier in the day by a captain from Corps showing rendezvous areas for these divisions. Now, because of later information on the situation, the divisions had to go into defensive positions. Our communications with the area in the Bulge were very poor and our information was fragmented. In many cases, lines had been cut or units with switchboards had been captured. The Germans had penetrated our area much further than earlier reported. He said, "You will meet Capt. Jones at this location and whatever you do, treat this map with care. It must not fall into enemy hands. This headquarters will arrive about midday tomorrow." If I were to get lost, captured, or chicken out, much could be lost. Only later on did I realize the magnitude of the responsibility placed in my hands at that moment. Somehow I don't think Colonel Barnes realized it at this time, either. It was all very low key—just a job to be done.

That evening marked one of the longest and loneliest drives in my life. I was charged with taking this marked map from our Kornielimunster, Germany, Corps headquarters to a crossroads town in Belgium called Havalange and there meeting the forward elements of the 83rd and 84th Infantry Divisions and the 2nd Armored Division, showing them the front to be established to block the German Panzer Divisions driving into Belgium. I was, of course, to advise the captain who had preceded me of the reason for this change. My driver and I left in the late afternoon with heavy clouds and light, wet snow falling, and drove toward Liège as darkness fell and the snow got heavier. All units had been alerted to expect Germans in American uniforms, and any lone soldier was suspect. Passwords were changed in each unit's area and clever MPs would ask identities of baseball players and baseball history as a substitute for password identification. Not being a fan of all this, I knew none! We were grilled many times, actually taken into custody, and had numerous pistols and rifles shoved in our faces that night. We did enough fast talking to last a lifetime. As we passed the Liège railroad yards V-1 and V-2 rockets landed, blowing up trains (and we learned later, our Christmas presents from home) adding to the nightmare.

Around 11:00 P.M., we arrived at what I determined to be our objective—Havalange. Just a cluster of stone buildings and no people! The captain was not there, and I was certain he had been killed or captured. I paced back and forth on that road junction from 11:00 P.M. until 2:00 A.M. the next morning in the cold and snow while my driver slept peacefully in the Jeep! At last the forward party of the 3rd Armored Division arrived. I was greatly relieved as their vehicles materialized out of the dark, blowing snow to identify them as friendly. I had been instructed to advise these parties to get their units in the defensive positions outlined on the map as soon as practicable. Everything possible was to be done to expedite that placement.

An amusing little episode developed, there in the pre-dawn darkness. I explained the tactical situation to this particular party and showed them the marked up map. They suggested that I go with them to point out their exact location and area of responsibility. I told them that I was by myself and that I had other units coming in. They were on their own. After some grumbling, they allowed "as to how" if a representative of Corps didn't feel inclined to venture on down that road, they were damned if they were going until some of their main body arrived at daybreak. They had half-tracks and a dozen and a half well-armed men. I found this attitude to exist on several occasions. The assumption was that a representative of higher headquarters had more knowledge of the situation than he was relating and you were safer to stick with him. Flattering, but not always the case. As it developed, fate was on their side and the enemy was a lot closer than any of us had imagined. The forward parties of the 83rd and 84th Infantry Divisions arrived by 4:30 and this phase of my mission was complete. As these forward parties moved off at daybreak on the road to Marche, they encountered the German Panzer Division forward parties within two miles, coming in our direction! A firefight of several hours developed until more of the 3rd Armored forces arrived.

The Corps officer with whom I was to meet put in an appearance about midday. It developed, after some questioning, that this captain had stopped in Liège to pay a social call on some chick whom he had met some weeks before. He had decided it wouldn't be safe to go on to Havalange in the dark! He had spent some time during the previous weeks "improving" our relations with this particular buxom Belgique. This career officer was removed from Corps forthwith and sent back to the States. End of career! Aside from the career loss, I thought many times in the days and nights that followed that being sent back to the States was not a bad deal at all!

Being appointed a combat liaison officer gives you a great deal of freedom of action and freedom from supervision in the field. If you're dedicated to the job, it's adventuresome, frightening at times, and very satisfying. If you're not dedicated, and always there are those who aren't, there is almost unlimited opportunity to satisfy a thirst for booty such as guns, booze, cameras, and women.

Our VII Corps forward arrived piecemeal later on the 22nd, and we were operational by the end of the day. I was much relieved to see them, and dog tired. By this time I had gone for over thirty-six hours without rest and with only cold food. I did get some hot coffee and some Spam warmed up on the manifold of my jeep. The cold and tension of the responsibility was driving me to my knees. At last I found some hay in a shed, wrapped myself in my bedroll, and asked a friend to wake me when the war was over.

Early on the 23rd Monty pulled in to take a look and to consult with General Collins and his staff. The hasty layout of the new Corps headquarters was more informal than usual, and I found myself, along with a couple of other junior officers, unintentionally boxed into what served as a map room when Monty made his unannounced entrance. Suddenly, there he was, in his sheepskin-lined flight jacket and black beret. Monty wasted no time—just a brief greeting to General Collins, then a request for "a sit rep" as of that morning. He then advised General Collins of the strength on his right and left flanks, and all available intelligence on what we faced. Finally, he asked for General

Collins's evaluation of his division's capabilities and his recommendation. General Collins replied, "Sir, I don't have enough supplies, food, ammunition, and gasoline to survive a withdrawal, nor an extended holding action. I must attack as soon as my troops are set." Visibly pleased with the answer, Monty promptly gave his approval. He said, "I'm taking the 75th Division off the 'red ball' duty, and giving them to you. You also get the 3rd Armored back again."

While I have no desire to tarnish Ike's great image, I must observe that we never saw him up front in VII Corps area during the thick of battle. Informal information from officers coming up from Paris was that Ike and his staff were holed up in their hotel under heavy security, concerned that the Germans might pull a sneak attack attempting to capture the staff. Monty, on the other hand, was out and much in evidence as the battle progressed.

"Red ball" duty was resupply, trucking food, ammunition, gasoline, and other supplies from the beachhead to the front. The designated "red ball" units had priority on all roads. The 75th had not yet seen combat. The 75th Division staff, acting as forward party, did arrive in a day or so. I once again was given a marked map showing their rendezvous area and ordered to escort the party there. I was also provided with notes on other information and a sealed message to their commanding general. It was probably a personal message of welcome from General Collins to their CG and instructions for a Corps staff meeting to follow. The general and his staff were friendly and obviously excited at the prospect of getting off the road and into the fray. We toured their general area and I answered as many questions as I could, feeling important briefing a general and his staff. Finally, the general turned to his staff officers and said, "Our people will be starting to arrive at 1400 hours.

Get their areas marked and get them under cover in those woods and dug in by dark." I said, "Excuse me, sir, but if you go into the woods, start cutting timber right away to cover their trenches or foxholes. Every shell the Krauts fire is an airburst first, in effect, when you're in the woods. Open trenches would be murder. You're safer in the trenches in the field until you can arrange cover." The general said, "OK, Lieutenant, we'll remember that. Anything else you wish to contribute?" I replied, "Well, sir, I picked up from conversations this afternoon that your antitank capability is all towed guns, not self-propelled. I will pass this information on to the Corps right away." The G3 broke in and said, "We learned in Louisiana maneuvers that towed pieces are more effective. They can be placed where self-propelled units can't go." I replied, "Check it with our G3, sir. I suspect you'll find he has some other thoughts on that subject." Later he did check this out, and our Colonel Troxel showed him the errors in his thinking and assigned self-propelled antitank units to the 75th. I felt pretty good about all this. They still didn't give me my own division, though!

The Corps set up road blocks, repulsed numerous enemy thrusts, and consolidated its position, and by 26 December was inflicting very heavy losses on the enemy. We found that our mines were not effective against their Tiger tanks, nor were their own 9-pound Teller mines. But stacked Teller mines were. They laughed at our mines. It was discouraging to sit in a defensive position from time to time and watch the enemy tanks come at you through your own mine fields as they popped harmlessly under their tracks. With heavy cloud cover, our Air Corps was useless. Under these circumstances, our field artillery was called upon again and again. A hit by our 155s was very effective and even the great Tiger tanks bit the dust. Our bazookas were much too light to do the job on the Tigers, except from the rear. Our 4.2-inch chemical mortars placed within range of road junctions and where tanks were apt to halt in defilade proved to be a fine antitank weapon. This weapon, unlike the conventional smooth-bore mortar, had rifling in the barrel and thus the capability of being quite accurate. Firing from behind snow banks and bushes, these crews could, and did, place rounds in open hatches of tanks at rest on several occasions.

Fighting in bitter weather, Corps troops by 27 December had retaken Humain. By 29 December contact had been made with the XVIII and XXX Corps, and the perimeter of a pocket was beginning to form.

There were many nights of terror in Normandy and on other occasions as we went along, in particular those snowy nights during the Bulge when we were under attack by an enemy—the best the Nazis had left and in their death throes. Their commanding officers knew they had nothing to lose and everything to gain. As shells rained down on us in whatever stone building we could find in this snowy Belgian landscape, each man turned inward for whatever strength he could find. My strength came from my faith that I brought with me. The 23rd Psalm was frequently in my mind and on my lips—had been all along and continued to be. It served me well. It kept me on my feet instead of cowering in a corner.

From time to time I would receive information regarding the activities of my old outfit, the 951st Field Artillery Battalion—frequently of the harrowing experiences; always of their efficiency and heroism under fire. One day word came of one of those tragedies that seemed to stand out. My old friend Lieutenant White, the pilot of one of the battalion's Piper Cubs, had been killed—not by enemy fire and not by taking unnecessary chances, but by heroically avoiding another Cub, slipping his into the ground. I was told this happened on the last day of December. Our Piper Cub planes performed some amazing feats, such as landing and taking off from dogleg roads and taking off from fields too small for proper operation. They would rev up the motor with brakes on and ground crew holding the wings, let go and race to the far side of the field, take off and stall just over the hedgerow, bounce down in the next adjacent field and continue on their run, finally gaining flying speed. It seems Lt. White was performing a somewhat similar maneuver when, without his knowledge, a fellow pilot was doing the same thing over the hedge in the contiguous field. The second pilot appeared under White at a crucial point and without sufficient air speed to get away. White side-slipped away and into the ground. He lost his life on the spot. I had flown many times with him in the States and in England, only twice on the continent, and I mourned the loss.

The massacre of the eighty-six or so field artillery observation battalion soldiers near Malmédy enraged us all. Captured by the enemy at the outset of the Bulge drive, they were lined up in a snowy field and machine-gunned to death. The Germans only created problems for themselves by that atrocity. We needed captured troops for interrogation, but they always seemed to try to "escape" and were shot in the attempt. Additionally, our troops fought with greater determination than ever before.

The German 88 started off life as a standard, high-velocity antiaircraft gun. On an ad hoc basis but with deadly effect it was used to knock out French bunkers in 1940. It then became an antitank weapon, the deadliest of the entire war. It was then mounted on their Tiger tanks and was the dreaded scourge from Normandy to the Bulge and after. At the height of the battle in the Bulge, I encountered a gruesome sight: four tank destroyers dug in, hull down with only the gun turrets above the ground, in an ideal position to pick off any tanks coming over the ridge to their front. Each tank had its turret blown cleanly off. They had been the victims of the tough Tiger tank with its accurate 88mm high-velocity gun.

Our only answer to those early overcast days was field artillery and 4.2-inch mortars. Our forward observers would lie in wait in snow banks for hours until tanks passed near a previously located checkpoint and then phone a firing order to a battery over the hills behind them. The overcast conditions robbed us of air cover we so desperately needed. We had few hills for distant observation so fire control was from trees or building ruins along the way. Our forward observers had to have a keen eye and ultimate faith in their battery commanders to conduct fire practically in their laps.

The British too had a similar, if not more deadly, weapon in their armory: a 3.5-inch antiaircraft gun that actually outranged the 88. This had been used in Tobruk with deadly effect. Because of the War Office rivalry between various branches, its development had been discouraged and it was not seen in the field in the ETO.

On 3 January the First U.S. Army resumed the offensive with the VII Corps making the main effort. In spite of intense cold and extensive minefields, it made good progress. On 13 January all divisions of the Corps attacked, cutting the German supply route between Houfalize and St. Vith and capturing Laroche as well as other towns. Contact was made with the Third Army elements at Laroche. Fighting during this period was very intense, but the tide had changed and VII Corps troops made steady but bitterly won progress.

At one point, two companies of troops were surrounded in a small village. They were out of communication with their regiment and presumed killed or captured. Ammunition for their heavy weapons and guns had been expended and food had run out a day or so before. A tough decision had to be made. They could surrender or try to sneak out under cover of darkness and a light snowfall. They lacked even enough rifle ammunition to stage a desperate attack. The officers and noncoms made the wounded as comfortable as possible, gave those who requested it a grenade in case they chose that way out, and filed silently out in the dark and snow. They followed fence and wall lines across fields all night and got back to our lines without attracting any attention. I don't recall the name of the unit. With the intelligence information they provided, an attack was mounted and shortly the town was taken. None of us slept that night as plans were made.

In the final reckoning, artillery and rocket-firing planes had saved the day as tank after tank was destroyed. The Allies lost 80,000 dead, wounded, or prisoners of war in the action. The Germans lost 120,000. On a tank-for-tank faceoff, we were outgunned. Our tanks had neither the guns nor the armor to match the Tigers. With their wide treads, the Tigers could float even their heavy armor over soft soil. We won by unorthodox means—i.e., planes and artillery plus numbers of tanks to "swarm" over them.

Throughout the period of 22 December through most of January, I was constantly doing liaison work between units of the 2nd Armored Division, the 75th Infantry Division, and Corps headquarters. My task was to keep Corps headquarters informed of the progress and/or problems of the units to which I was assigned. I spent many hours on the road. The night runs were particularly harrowing. A few inches of snow and a lack of traffic to make reference tracks left one in "whiteout ground conditions." Where exactly is the road? Where are the ditches? Is this the mined area I have been warned about? Damn those blackout lights! Another couple of inches of snow and we'll have to stop and shovel out the Jeep and start over. So finally you got back to Corps at midnight and there is information to take back to division—now! And it starts all over. By the end of January I was so damned tired I wouldn't have ducked if the enemy had pointed a gun right in my face. Finally it was over and I just wanted to sleep for a month. How many others must have shared my feelings?

As with all stressful situations, the Battle of the Bulge brought out the best and the worst in men. I am proud to say I saw the best in our men many times. As I have said, my job required me to make many night runs over poorly marked roads with the fresh snow cover. I was working with the 2nd Armored Division. My only radio link back to Corps was through their radio in an armored half-track commanded by a big fellow by the name of Major King. His crew was composed of several soldiers and noncommissioned officers from the Bronx. A great group. They insisted that I bunk down with them and sort of make my base of operations at their equipment. A most welcome situation under the circumstances. They had taken over a stone outbuilding in a farm cluster that was division headquarters. The building looked great. But they found it had been occupied by a German outpost in a last ditch stand. The Germans were either too frightened or too lazy to go outside to relieve themselves and had used a pile of hay in one corner of the building for that purpose. Well, our guys cleaned it out and set up their equipment, as well as a heater. As soon as the temperature got above 50 degrees the odor was overwhelming. At this juncture I had to make a trip to Corps that was early in the evening and did not return until after dawn.

When I did return the soldier on guard greeted me with a laugh and said, "Lieutenant, you are in for a real treat."

I said, "I can hardly wait. I bet it stinks like hell in there."

"Well, not like you would think. Go in and have a smell."

I opened the door and was greeted with the darnedest mixture of odors you ever encountered. The guys had heated the place up and then aired it out. Next they had brought in brooms and water with GI soap and finally several of them brought out bottles of perfume that they'd bought for their wives on unauthorized visits to Paris. They had mixed this with water and scrubbed the place out all over again. It was amazing! Later that morning the sergeant explained "We couldn't have a guest from Corps tell everyone the 2nd Armored stunk, Lieutenant, so we had to do this."

These fellows shared their food packages from home with me on several occasions. This included packages one mother had sent with a large-size can of "pineapple juice." It seemed to me that this was a funny thing to send. All the crew encouraged me to think this. Then when they had me duped into being the straight man they told me this was just one of many cans his mother had sent. We all sat down around the heater and they broke out some enameled cups, punctured the can and poured us each a hearty shot of bourbon!! Then they peeled off the label of the "pineapple juice" can to reveal a patch of solder on one side. That Italian mother would do anything to make her son happy.

Mines blew tracks off tanks and half-tracks on many occasions. They also rolled them over. Our tanks suffered this indignity, as did the German medium tanks. Crews would then be trapped inside. When the tanks were punctured, ammunition and fuel would be set afire. I was sickened to see and smell this. Removal of bodies from these burned out vehicles was an unenviable task.

For the first time since it had crossed the Seine River in August, the Corps on 24 January was without contact with the enemy and without a front line. For us, the "Battle of the Bulge" was over. An unfortunate aftermath of the battle was Monty's boastful claim of full credit for winning the battle. This caused Patton and Bradley to threaten resignation until Churchill smoothed things over in a speech to the House of Commons, calling the Bulge the greatest American battle of the war in Europe. The American soldier in Europe came of age in this battle and in that of the Hurtgen Forest, as his brothers in the South Pacific did there.

As we settled into rest camp, with troops just glad to have survived, weapons cleaning was one of the first orders of the day. A good commander, from division on down to squad, always required this cleaning, knowing that immediate action is a possibility even if not a probability. Troops are always taught that there is no such thing as an unloaded weapon unless the bolt is back and you can see an open chamber. Nevertheless, as the rest period had just started, we were saddened to have one of the division troops shoot his buddy and kill him with an "empty" gun.

Considering the thousands who were lost in this action, this would seem to be insignificant. It was not. The lad who pulled the trigger and his buddy were both casualties. All of us who got the report in the first few hours were casualties.

From 25 January to 4 February all units of the VII Corps remained in rest areas. On 5 February the Corps moved back to Germany to take over its former zone along the Roer River. After we pulled out of Belgium and returned to our positions in Germany, we read in *The Stars and Stripes* of Gen. Tony McAuliffe's response to the German general who demanded his surrender of the 101st Division at Bastogne. We were quite amused at the article. We knew the general, and knew people who were there on that occasion. His response was not one word ("Nuts!") but two, and a bit less suited for home newspaper consumption. We were highly amused to visualize the task the messenger had of taking the message back to the German general. When the general asked him what was the response, he had to say, "Sir, McAuliffe's response is '——— you!'" That must have been quite an embarrassing job.

In early February, I had a temporary respite from my duties and decided to take advantage of the situation and try to locate and visit some of my old friends. One was a high school classmate, now Capt. Wayne Pierce, Company Commander, 101st Airborne. Correspondence from my sister, Betty, made frequent mention of her friend Wilma Pierce, and of her husband who was in the 101st Airborne. I was intrigued by all of this. Wayne and his brothers were quiet, well-scrubbed, religious, scholarly, and gentle young fellows in our school days. Certainly not macho or militaristic in any way. What kind of an Airborne trooper would Wayne be? How successful would this gentle guy be as a leader of some of this Army's toughest soldiers? I made inquiries through my fellow liaison officers until I located his unit, and one day drove to his command post. His unit had been pulled back to a rest area. When I arrived at a shed that served as his "dayroom," he was out performing some company business, but expected back shortly. I introduced myself to his noncommissioned officers and in chatting with them mentioned that this was such a gentle guy in school that I was surprised to see him in such an aggressive outfit. That comment opened a flood of comments from the three or four enlisted men there. Captain Pierce was obviously a much-admired leader. They all held him in high esteem. They counted on his wisdom and judgment. Above all, they admired his aggressive bravery. One sergeant said, "Sir, when we get pinned down by enemy machine gunners and the rest of us are trying to get as far into the ditch as possible, the Captain will grab his gun and walk right down the middle of the road firing as he goes and goes after them. You just have to follow a guy like that!" Wayne returned shortly and we enjoyed a brief visit until I had to return to my unit. He was and still is the same gentle gentleman today. His faith has never failed him. You just know he had a short intensive conversation with God before he took off down that road each time!

X
The Push to the Rhine

The date was 20 February, 1945, and there was an air of expectancy in the headquarters. A truck had arrived with America's secret weapon. Case after case of Coca-Cola!!! The first since England. Over a year and a half! Now we each had two bottles of warm Coca-Cola. I drank one and gave the other away.

After a long period of intense preparation, the Corps attacked across the Roer River at Düren on 23 February with the 9th Infantry Division on the right and the 104th Infantry Division on the left. "Intense preparation" in this case meant hundreds of fighter bomber runs and thousands of rounds of heavy and medium artillery for weeks. I had never seen a city so pulverized. In spite of all this, the Germans crawled from basement to basement through holes cut in common foundation walls. They fought back for every building and for every block. Our troops were ferried across the river in boats under cover of heavy smoke, and by the end of the day had taken two towns and cleared the northern part of artillery-battered Düren. One of the few remaining building walls was a three-story wall of the telephone exchange building. I was amused to see the large switchboard still attached to the remaining third floor wall. Also by the end of the day, the first of five bridges was in place.

One of the few remaining recognizable items on the landscape here in Düren was in what had been one of the town's parks. It was a slightly larger than life-size statue of Bismarck mounted on a horse. He had been facing west looking toward Alsace of the much coveted Alsace-Lorraine area. The Germans had always wanted this area, and took it back from France when they could. Now old Bismarck seemed to be the only survivor of another war, but there was a surprise. The statue was equipped with a long threaded rod running from head to the base. This secured the cast statue in place, and in spite of the nearby bomb and shell bursts, it worked. The ironic aspect of all this was that Bismarck's neck had been broken by the concussion. His head now faced east—away from Alsace. That conquest will still have to wait another generation or so.

Once inside Germany, many soldiers experienced an increased interest in learning some German. My old outfit, the 951st Field Artillery Battalion, enjoyed telling of the experience of one of their members who was standing around waiting for the signal for his unit to move out. He suddenly felt the call of nature, grabbed a shovel and a roll of paper, and moved into the edge of the woods for privacy. He dug a hole, took down his pants, and was in the midst of doing his duty when he looked up and there a few yards in front of him were three German soldiers coming out of the woods carrying their weapons. Our artillery man had learned a few German phrases, so he grabbed his trousers, pulled them up, and while he held them in one hand grabbed his carbine with the other and shouted in the best German he could muster, "Drop your weapons or I'll shoot." The Germans looked at him, dropped their guns, and broke into gales of laughter. Only later did our guy learn that he didn't quite get the "shoot" right, and friend and foe enjoyed a moment of levity at his expense.

Düren, at that time the second-largest city to fall to the Allied armies in the west, was captured by VII Corps on 24

February. From there the drive swept rapidly across the Cologne plain, and a bridgehead across the Erft canal was established 28 February.

We were told that the Ford Motor plant north of Cologne was in operation up to the day we took it. Further, it was in communication with Detroit up to that time. This did not set too well with any of us. Strict orders were issued to the Air Force and to all ground forces to spare the Cologne Cathedral all possible damage. For the most part this was carried out. The Germans did not use it as a strong point.

Elements of the Corps reached the Rhine in strength at Worrington, 4 March, and entered Cologne on 5 March. Fifty-seven hours later the city, third-largest in Germany, fell to VII Corps. Bonn, a city with a population of more than 100,000, fell to VII Corps on 9 March.

My driver at this stage was a former race-car driver and was a bit wild from time to time. He did make me nervous and I would caution him. One morning he said, "Lieutenant, I know you have a bad back and don't feel too comfortable in the Jeep, but when you caution me most of the time I'm about to do just what you say to do. I hope you don't think I'm insubordinate, but you make me nervous."

I said, "OK, we'll try it your way. No offense taken—you're probably right." We were headed for the town of Bad Gadesberg over a two-lane highway that hugged a long range of hills. Steep hills on our right, steep drop-off on the left with trees spaced every fifty feet on a ten-foot shoulder. The road was sheltered from the sun from time to time. Water stood in the road. We were sandwiched into an armored column that was not moving at a constant speed and my driver was working his way forward far too aggressively when we wheeled around a curve, hit a patch of water, and skidded sideways. Our trailer jackknifed, shoving us out of control. First we headed for the churning tracks of a tank and then for the shoulder and the 50- to 75-foot cliff! As we slid sideways I could see we were going to take one of the trees right in my side. I instinctively put out my hand, then pulled it back and grabbed the tube base of the seat just as we impacted the tree! The Jeep wound up with a funny shape. Our trailer rolled over with the contents all over the road. I had a ringing in my head from my helmet hitting the tree with my head in it! And for days I was sore all up one side. My driver lost his cool and, pounding on the Jeep with his fists, just kept saying, "I'm sorry, Lieutenant. I'm sorry, I'm sorry, I'm sorry!" I said, "Enough of that. Let's pick up my stuff off the road and get out of here. We're holding up a whole armored column."

The guys in the armored column quickly dismounted and to my surprise helped clean up the mess, righted the trailer, and then hooked a cable to the rear of the Jeep, whose front wheels had started over the edge of the cliff but were held back by the tree imbedded in our side.

That evening the motor sergeant asked who I would like for a new driver. I said, "I'll keep the one I have. I think he has probably learned a lesson."

He said, "No, he feels so guilty and nervous that he wants a new job."

I knew his major concern was that if I made the report he deserved they would give him a rifle and send him to the infantry. Replacements were always needed.

On 5 March, American Armies began their race to cross the Rhine, Hodges' First Army to the North and Patton's Third Army to the South. Patton is said to have exclaimed that if he lost this race he would be "most ashamed." He lost the race. When elements of the 9th Armored Division, III Corps, found a partially intact railroad bridge at Remagen, they crossed over the great river barrier. The relatively new

III Corps was the corps on our right flank. I was the liaison officer from VII Corps to III Corps on the exciting night of this action and was in the III Corps war room. All present were instructed to not mention the taking of the bridge in reports to their units. I knew General Collins wanted to cross the Rhine in our sector, but he was being held back by First Army. I also knew my hide would be nailed to the wall if I were to be caught sending this information to General Collins. Nevertheless, using an alphabet code, I called VII Corps on the land line and gave my normal report on unit positions in the vicinity of our common line. I worked in a coordinate description that showed troops over the Rhine in the vicinity of the bridge at Remagen. This went undetected by the III Corps staff.

My superiors at VII Corps sent a terse message back asking if I had checked my data, to which I replied in the affirmative. General Collins advised First Army headquarters and asked permission to cross in the vicinity of Bonn. Army shot a message to III Corps asking verification and an explanation on why they had not been informed. All this in the space of thirty minutes. III Corps was still trying to decide what code form to use to send this highly sensitive information back to Army while VII Corps was released to begin bridge-building and crossing operations immediately.

I was certain my next report would be from the brig. I stayed up all night dispatching other messages to my corps on positions of minor units, hoping my violating message would get lost in the shuffle. It did and I heard nothing of it.

Part of being a successful liaison officer was the development of a sixth sense that told you as you watched the troop movement along the front that events—big or at least unusual—were about to happen. I had that feeling that night and while my fellow liaison officers went to hit the sack or go souvenir hunting I stayed up for no reason I could articulate. It paid off. I had a constant fear that I would oversleep some night and when I rolled out in the morning someone would say, "Hey, Maxey, the war was lost last night while you were sleeping." I knew I had Ike to fall back on, but I felt responsible.

As can be imagined, the excitement at III Corps and VII Corps over the unexpected good fortune of finding a marginally usable bridge over the Rhine was only exceeded by the gut-wrenching reaction on the part of the enemy. They had counted on defending the Rhine line at all costs and it was now breached.

As was the case with all bridges of any size in Europe, pockets had been built into the structure of adequate size and location to contain explosives for demolition, should the occasion warrant it. This ability to demolish bridges was utilized routinely by the retreating Germans. In the case of the Remagen railroad bridge, one block of explosives functioned as planned, cutting the lower tension cord of the structure and leaving the bridge bed tilted at a precarious angle. The other block did not explode and the cord held, but was greatly overstressed. The engineers worked frantically to strengthen this weakened portion of the bridge while foot soldiers crossed cautiously on the other side, undoubtedly praying all the way. Meanwhile, artillery fire against the enemy side of the embankment kept their heads down. Engineers rushed pontoon-bridge-building equipment to the site and frantic hours were spent building a floating bridge near the damaged one. We all knew that the life of the railroad bridge was probably limited.

The Germans fought back with all they had. Gunfire from the far shore was intense, making the gathering of information on the progress of various units not only difficult but hazardous. Our antiaircraft filled the sky with tracers, and their success in bringing down enemy planes only added to the peril on the ground. Exploding bombs and planes were like a three-ring circus.

Antiaircraft batteries of all calibers were rushed to this area. Concentric rings of guns were formed, smaller caliber close to the bridge and larger caliber farther out. And the German air force came! Suicide dives at the troops and at the bridge, which had to be destroyed at all cost! The sight by day, but particularly by night, of this concentration of antiaircraft fire, the greatest since D-Day, was more thrilling than any Fourth of July fireworks. It was unforgettable. But keep your helmet on and your head down, it is raining lead. Finally, V-2 rockets rained down. Interestingly enough, no bombs actually hit the bridge, but the concussion was enough to shake the tired and injured old structure and after a few days it gave up and failed. The bridge gave us plenty of warning as it sagged. I looked at it and felt it could go any time. At this time I had had no engineering training, so my opinion was based on intuition. All I could say was that I would "wait and take the pontoon, if you don't mind." Unfortunately, several of the III Corps engineers on the bridge went with it. By this time, the pontoon bridge was in place and troops and weapons were streaming across to the other side, creating a bridgehead and attacking the enemy. Just my luck! No film for my camera. My film all came from bombed-out stores in the various towns along the way, so my supply was not too constant.

Our bridge-building efforts were quite successful—we bridged the Rhine just south of Cologne in ten hours, providing access for tanks and heavy trucks. There was always the need for more bridging. Our engineers solved this problem on one occasion by commandeering a group of Rhine River barges. They tied them firmly together and secured bridging track from deck to deck, and we had a more satisfactory heavy-duty bridge. River traffic was at a standstill anyway, so this barrier had no effect on that.

It was at this time that I was called back to Corps headquarters for a conference with Colonel Carter, our G-2 (intelligence) officer. He advised me that General Collins had resisted having a public relations officer. He didn't want glory for himself, but now realized that he was shortchanging the personnel in the Corps' subordinate units. He wanted to appoint a Corps PRO to rectify this and get word back to hometown papers about their boys. He had further decided I was it! I was well known throughout the Corps and could start operations without a lot of introductions, according to Carter. My protestations that I really lacked the credentials, both in education and in experience that the job required, didn't faze him. (I still suspect that General Palmer had a hand in all this.) I was to get the full cooperation of S-2 (personnel) in a search for a noncommissioned officer with journalistic background, and I could take my pick. Further, I was advised that as we moved from one location to another, the General and his immediate staff would, of course, be provided with the best facilities and I was to get the next pick. This was all designed so that I could host the war correspondents and other visiting dignitaries, whom we anticipated now would come in at the end of the war, in the best possible style. If I needed anything else, I was to ask for it. Most of all, I was to get those stories out to the hometown newspapers. I was a bit breathless at all this, but plunged in. After a week, fate brought me together with a sergeant who had been a professor of journalism at Iowa State College, and we were on our way. So now I'm a public relations officer, of all things! I felt like the recruit assigned to the engineers who wrote home to tell his family, "This Army is really great! Imagine! Yesterday I couldn't even spell enguineer, and today I are one!" Sergeant Fox and I cranked out stories in great style. Most were not too thrilling, but the folks at home appreciated their boys' names in print. The war correspondents who visited our offices seemed to appreciate our cooperation and at the culmination of hostilities, I was awarded a Bronze Star for my efforts in this department.

By this time, I was being provided with excellent facilities and quarters. My office for the several days we were in Bonn was a second-floor apartment overlooking the Rhine River. It was beautifully furnished, and the view was great. We churned out dozens of stories for hometown paper consumption.

The war correspondents accredited to First Army were an interesting lot. Many were walking history books capable of recalling relevant events in history or in literature as they wrote their dispatches of the moment. These were correspondents such as the *Chicago Tribune*'s John Thompson, who was the first paratroop correspondent; Hal Boyle and Don Whitehead of the Associated Press; Martha Gelhorn, Ernest Hemingway's wife; Richard C. Hottelet of CBS; and some fifty others.

As Corps Public Relations Officer, it was my assignment to host the war correspondents covering events throughout VII Corps area. The summit staff meeting at Kur Hotel in Petersburg, Germany, on 26 March, was one such event. I arranged for food and drink, which was served on the hood of my Jeep while Ike, Bradley, Hodges, and Collins dined inside and conferred. One of the enterprising correspondents got into the hotel office and searched through the files for story material. He found unpaid bills from a previous high-level conference—they were the bills run up by American foreign correspondents at the famous "Peace in Our Time" conference between

Neville Chamberlain and Adolf Hitler. What an interesting turn of events.

The visitors did come. French officers, Chinese staff officers, and finally the politicians from Washington with their staffs when the shooting had finally stopped. We could just imagine their "expert" testimonies when they returned to Washington. They had *been* there! We called them "carpetbaggers." Later on, in college on the GI Bill, we had an economics professor who started referring to his brother, who had been in Germany after the war, and a fellow veteran sitting next to me turned and in a not-too-soft voice said, "Oh, another carpetbagger." Our prof turned red in the face and stomped out of the class.

XI
The Final Stage

Corps elements (1st Division) crossed the Rhine to the Remagen bridgehead 15 March. On 16 March, the 78th Division expanded the bridgehead. Both divisions attacked 17 March to expand the First Army bridgehead. This first bridge in VII Corps area was constructed under cover of a heavy smokescreen to frustrate enemy attempts to knock it out. Still, it was completed in a record ten hours—perhaps cheered on by the Red Cross girls serving coffee and doughnuts right there as the engineers worked in the smoke. Construction of the second Rhine bridge was begun 18 March, and construction of the third bridge was begun 20 March. With the Rhine bridged at so many points, our troops were pouring east and once more the feeling of exhilaration abounded. By 21 March the bridgehead in the VII Corps area was extended to the Sieg River.

The command post of the VII Corps opened at Konigswinter at 1600 hours on 22 March, thus becoming the first operational U.S. Corps headquarters east of the Rhine.

In spite of a change from limited delaying action to heavy fighting on the part of the enemy, the Corps captured Altankirchen on 25 March, crossed the Dill River on 27 March, and captured Marburg on 28 March.

Some evenings there was an artificial sun as whole towns burned a few miles in front of us. The sky was aglow with the fires. From time to time searchlights were brought up, turned on, and directed at the overhanging clouds. This gave a soft light that would frustrate infiltrators; however, it also exposed our patrols.

Armored units of the VII Corps advanced to the north to reach several points below Paderborn and virtually encircled the enemy forces in the Ruhr from the north and east. On 31 March, enemy forces in the Ruhr pocket were nearly cut off and entrapped during the day as VII Corps units operating on the southern and eastern sides of the pocket strengthened their long line extending eastward along the Sieg River from its junction with the Rhine to the vicinity of Siegen and northeastward to the vicinity of Paderborn. The capture of Paderborn was no small feat. It was the Fort Knox and Fort Sill of Germany, the armored school with artillery ranges all marked out. Enemy tanks were very familiar with every hill and dale. They treated our appearance on the scene as just another school problem, and we were the targets.

March 31st and April 1st marked another period of great tension. At VII Corps, the pocket formed south of Paderborn consisted of a single line of regular troops plus administrative personnel. General Collins really sweated this out. Some of us from Corps headquarters went out for a couple of days to man some positions along the Sieg River. Fortunately, the enemy did not know the situation and didn't counterattack.

A fascinating discovery took place in early spring when we encountered what at first appeared to be a rather Spartan country hotel. There was a series of private rooms comfortably furnished, a large lounge area, an exercise room, and dining facilities. A fair-sized swimming pool and a large open deck were included. A rest area for tired soldiers? Well, sort of. The walls held photographs of Afrika Corps soldiers looking fit and very German. Other photos showed buxom German girls. The records in the medical dispensary told the story. This was a breeding pen intended to provide the next generation of "pure" Aryans. These were to be soldiers for future war machines. According to our interrogators, some of the youngest POWs we captured already looked upon Hitler as their father. Those were the "Hitler Jungen." From these facilities would come some real fanatics in the future.

March was a great month in many ways, but our exhilaration was tempered when we lost Maj. Gen. Maurice Rose, commander of the U.S. 3rd (Spearhead) Division. He was a superior tactician and a fine soldier, revered by his officers and men. I had found him most cooperative, both in my liaison work and later in my PRO work. I had first met him while serving with General Palmer. I always entertained the pleasant thought of seeing the day when this great Jewish fighter would have the pleasure of meeting Hitler, the Jew Killer. It never happened, of course. A machine gun got him as he moved with his tanks and the killer probably never knew he had killed a great man.

The 3rd Armored Division made a firm link-up with the Ninth Army at Lippstedt on 1 April to complete the encirclement of more than 350,000 German troops in the pocket. The 3rd Armored Division also captured Paderborn.

The Corps was relieved of its responsibilities along the perimeter of the pocket, and by 5 April started to attack to the east to secure crossings of the Weser River, which was accomplished by 8 April.

Against little opposition, armored units captured Nordhausen on 11 April and there uncovered an infamous concentration camp and a huge V-weapon plant hidden in a hillside. The capture of Nordhausen was not a great military action. Most enemy troops had fled the area, not wanting to be identified with this ghastly affair. But it proved to be one of the most emotional experiences of the war for our troops.

The town hosted two major installations, the Focke-Wolf Airplane Motor Factory and a tunnel holding a V-1 buzz bomb and a V-2 rocket factory. I had just started to set up my public relations office in the space allotted to me in our new headquarters when my driver burst through the door and said "Lt. Maxey, come with me please, sir. Bring your cameras. Please don't ask why. I can't explain it, but you'll see." This was a bit unmilitary and darned unusual, but it caught my imagination, so I followed along. He drove me to the edge of town and into the industrial area. As we entered the grounds of a factory I found myself looking at a sea of corpses. It was one of the most shocking experiences of my life. I understood why my driver could not tell me what to expect. Partially demolished factory buildings surrounded the vast concrete parking lot. Soldiers were bringing bodies out of the buildings. Some were placed in the ever-growing rows of dead. Some were taken to waiting ambulances and rushed away. As I walked to the building I was wading in a magnitude of death the likes of which I had never seen. There were 3,000 dead men, women, and children. In the end, there were also 3,000 survivors. As I surveyed this horrible sight I looked down at my feet and saw the body of a young girl. In her arms was a small doll. I looked again and realized that the doll was really a baby, probably a sibling.

I photographed the scene and put the pictures away because I couldn't look at them or discuss them for years without weeping. Weeping for the little girl and her sibling, weeping for the whole complex full of starved humans, weeping for those who perpetrated this heinous crime on humanity and their lost souls, weeping for a lethargic population that would tolerate prejudice as a little flame until it became an uncontrollable conflagration. I still have tears as I recall this sight!

The modus operandi was to work these people on minimum food until they could no longer fulfill their assigned tasks or became ill, then assign them to their bunks to starve. This was true in both the motor plant and the buzz bomb plant. The workers in the buzz bomb plant had the added "luxury" of working in the deep, damp tunnels, digging into the stone and breathing the dust without benefit of any protection. They soon developed respiratory problems and were discarded, awaiting death and cremation.

Sorting the living from the dead was a gruesome and emotional chore. Tough men were in constant tears. They had to be restrained from going into town and adding the locals to the pile at the factory. Common graves were dug on the grounds of a beautiful estate at the edge of town. General Collins ordered the Burgomeister to call all professionals, lawyers, doctors, engineers, clergy, businesspeople, and factory owners to attend a meeting in the town square dressed in their best. He then had our military police march them out to the factory site, to pick up these emaciated bodies by hand, place them on scraps of lumber with four men to each body, and take them up the hill to the mass graves. No hats allowed!

At a different location in Nordhausen, but nearby, was a large hill with an entrance leading to miles of underground tunnels complete with railroad tracks. Parts of V-1 and V-2 rockets lay in the storage yards and in the factory tunnels. Near the entrance was their crematorium. Neatly stacked nearby were the starved bodies of the slave laborers. Each body was marked with a long number similar to a social security number on an arm and across the belly.

Charts still hung on the wall showing progress in disposing of these bodies. Next door was a so-called hospital with box beds and a few live patients, abandoned by the fleeing staff. These patients were near starvation, but oh so happy to see us! They were immediately transported to our field hospital. I communicated with them as best I could, but had a hard time to keep from becoming very emotional.

We had quite a problem with our troops at that time because they all wanted to feed these people who were so near starvation. They had to be restrained because that was the worst thing they could do; it would kill them. Deliberately planned meals had to be given to them in order to nurse them back to life.

Later on, the summer of 1969, I had a fantastic experience. A construction worker on an apartment building in a Chicago suburb was introduced to me with the comment that, "I think the two of you have been in the same place during the war." The worker turned out to have been in Nordhausen when I was there in the so-called hospital at the buzz bomb plant, and we had seen each other at that time! There were only eight or ten live ones in those bunks. He had the identifying number on his arm (and, I suppose on his belly).

The stories the correspondents wrote that night were filled with emotion and references to other gruesome events in history, but concluded that this was, beyond all doubt, one of the worst crimes against humanity. These colorful and emotion-filled stories were edited and watered down by the publications' editors back home. The public never got to appreciate the excellent literature that was produced.

Resuming its attack to the east, the Corps took 2,200 prisoners of war to swell the total catch for the Corps to more than 200,000. By that time, all exits to the Hartz Mountain across to the south were blocked, and the 4th Cavalry Group entered the mountain area.

Upon hearing of President Roosevelt's death on 12 April 1945, the general atmosphere was of shock, with deep feelings of loss. It was like a combat loss. We felt he was a victim of this war. Truman was an unknown quantity to us. We just couldn't imagine a Missouri haberdasher taking over the reins of this gigantic enterprise with any success. In other words, we felt quite vulnerable. We could not be defeated in the field, but we could be from above. How wrong we were!

At this time I was receiving letters from stateside telling me of articles in various publications and speeches alerting the home folks to the problems they could expect with the returning soldiers. "These poor fellows, having lived in filth and with death for these many months, were most apt to be a bit dangerous. They have lost contact with their religion and their language will be most foul." When I became aware of all this I was at once amused and disgusted. Some writers will do anything to get a feature article in the papers. I wrote to Eva that I would do all in my power to keep the animal in me under control—at least for the first few minutes!

The Corps reached the Mulde River and entered Halle on 19 April. The city was captured 19 April. By 20 April, all organized resistance in the Hartz Mountains had ceased, and more than 18,000 prisoners were taken with nearly as many more still uncounted in regimental cages and in overrun military hospitals.

The town of Eisleben, the birthplace and for many years the home of Martin Luther, was relatively undamaged. I enjoyed visiting his church, seeing the font where he was baptized and the pulpit from which he proclaimed his theology of justification by faith. From here he was tried and excommunicated.

Our forward party had designated an apartment building as officers' quarters for a few days and it was pleasant to stay in civilized surroundings. I soon found the utilities were still in working order and on my second or third night arranged a party. I invited two of my fellow officers and three Red Cross girls to dinner. We arranged to draw our one-third ration (a ration is one day's food) for the six of us and had our first home-cooked meal in the apartment. We had an evening's conversation and then walked the girls back to their quarters. It was a nice interlude.

All resistance west of the Mulde River ended at 2100 on 22 April as the city of Dessau was cleared, and the Corps closed to the Mulde River along the entire Corps front.

At this stage in the game, Germans were fleeing the Russians and surrendering to American troops en masse. They came across the Muldi River and across the Elbe like rats leaving a sinking ship. They swam, they floated on pieces of furniture—one fellow I saw was on an ironing board—and anything else that would float. It was their heartfelt desire to be our prisoners rather than the Russians'. On numerous occasions, the request was made of us to arm them and let them join us to fight the Russians. "You will have to fight them eventually; why not now?" Speaking of the Russians, let it be said that they were an enigma to us. Once we had made contact with them, we assumed they would welcome their comrades whom we had picked up in Germany in PW pens and slave labor camps. We took this "comrade" business seriously and assumed they did too. Had they liberated Americans from PW or slave labor camps, we would have shared our rations and done everything in our power to stage a big "welcome home" party. Not so with the Russians. From their top commander (General Zdanov) on down, they were standoffish, suspicious, and very inhospitable. We had arranged for a trainload of their citizens to be brought to the front and turned over. We arrived at the appointed time and place and were told to take them back. "Perhaps tomorrow." Then the next day they would only take a few and delayed taking the rest. This "comrade" stuff was all bunk. We realized that we were the ones who looked upon our fellows as true comrades and we didn't need a political party to tell us when to do it!

The Corps command post moved to Leipzig on 30 April. General Collins hosted the Russian corps and army staffs on May 1st, a Russian holiday, his birthday, and also mine. It was quite a party! Over a dozen planes—artillery observation Piper Cubs and L-5 Corps liaison planes—were assigned the task of bringing the Russian staff officers from their command post east of the Elbe River to Leipzig. Our pilots got together and planned a little thrill for these unsmiling Russian staff officers. They flew over in formation in a very military fashion and landed in a designated area. Once all passengers were onboard, the planes took off and assembled at altitude—probably 4,000 feet. When they approached the Leipzig airport the planes peeled off one at a time, headed for the ground in a top-speed dive, pulled out a few feet from terra firma and climbed to a power-on stall, did a tailspin, recovered, and then swung back over the field. Some of those officers looked pretty peaked when they crawled out.

They brought reporters from TASS along with them to take pictures and write stories. As the party progressed, one of the TASS people offered me a cigarette. They were quite long as I recall, and I was curious, so I accepted. I tried to light the darn thing and was having problems. Like all cocktail parties, voices were getting louder and louder and there was much laughter. Suddenly, I became aware of the fact that the Russians, including their general, were laughing at me! Their cigarettes were three-quarters paper tube and one-quarter tobacco. I was attempting to light the tube. Our cigarettes up to that time were without filters and were the same at both ends. May I report that once lit, the cigarette was not worth the effort. Ours were better. At least I had the honor of giving a high ranking Russian general and his staff a good belly laugh.

As the afternoon wore on, two of the TASS officers asked for a tour of Leipzig. I got my Jeep and driver and we set off to see the sights. At last, one of them requested to see the monument to the defeat of Napoleon in 1813. We started out and got confused about the proper streets. German police were on duty as traffic cops, and we stopped to ask directions. This particular cop was less than cooperative, but my new TASS friend had a solution. He hopped out of the Jeep, grabbed the cop and sat him on the hood of my Jeep, and said in German, "Take us to the Napoleon monument—NOW!" By golly, he did.

Here we are in Leipzig in the Spring of 1945 all set for VE-Day. The lilacs are blooming in the parks and I come as close to being homesick as at any time in my four years and ten months in active service. All the troops—officers and men—are feeling that "now that the job is over, let's get packing and get home!"

The rule, strictly enforced, is "no fraternization." As I work at my desk on the ground floor of the Leipzig Fire Insurance Company building, I can see the MP security guard about seventy-five feet from my window and, through the open window, can catch snatches of conversation. I suddenly realize I am hearing girls' voices and laughter! This is war! Call out the troops! Line up the tanks! Unlimber the artillery! Our young MP is being attacked! Two young German girls are walking back and forth in front of this young man who is our guard. They are swinging their hips and patting their butts and saying "Verboten, ha ha ha, verboten." They are having a ball with our poor sex-starved young soldier! Our guard is bravely standing his ground. But what a story he had to tell his buddies that night!

May 8th was VE-day, an occasion for partying. General Collins invited his division commanders and General Zdonov, the Russian army commander, as well as several Russian division commanders, to a cocktail party and dinner at the Furstenhoff Hotel in Leipzig. The affair started off in good shape, but as usual the Russians hit the booze pretty hard.

Just as the guests were being called to take their places at the table, there was a commotion at the doorway and in marched a dozen and a half Russian MPs with machine guns at port arms. Their officer in charge instructed them to take up positions at intervals around the banquet hall. General Collins was incensed at this rude display of muscle. He called our provost marshal to his side and quietly instructed him to get an equal number of the biggest MPs armed with tommy guns and post them next to each Russian. He told our provost marshal if he didn't have enough large MPs, to quickly grab the biggest soldiers he could find and slap MP helmets on them and get them there on the double. What a pleasant atmosphere for a dinner!

As the dinner progressed, General Zdonov turned to a passing German waiter, and, pointing to his water glass, said, "Vasser." The waiter nodded and started to pass on.

The General reached out, grabbed the slim waiter by the back of his coat, and said, "I said 'vasser'!" He tugged so hard he threw him to the floor, causing him to drop his tray and its contents with a crash.

Finally, the dinner and speeches were over, and Zdonov leaned back from the table, patted his belly, and roared out, "Plenty to drink, plenty to eat, now I want a woman!" This was not General Collins's style. Here he was with a high-ranking, drunk, short-fused Russian general making obscene requests. What to do? He very wisely chose to make a joke of the request and hope for the best. After a few shaky moments, things calmed down and it came time for them to depart. Collins bid them Godspeed and breathed a sigh of relief!

On Wednesday, 30 May, 1945, a memorial service was scheduled for the newly established American cemetery at Eisenach, Germany. I decided to drive from Leipzig to the cemetery, and took my staff sergeant, Rodney Fox, along to cover the event. A portion of our route was on one of the German Autobahns, and we enjoyed the pleasant drive on a beautiful spring day.

The pleasantness of the day was tempered by our purpose: to visit the gravesites of so many of our comrades. Another distraction was the parade of displaced people lining each side of the highway, all headed home. Some pushed baby buggies and wheelbarrows, some pulled little wagons, and many carried bundles on their backs. All were trudging back to what was left of their homes. These were women and children, very young boys, and very old men.

As we drove along, we saw a flight of our twin-boomed P-38s fly over and then back, to line up with the highway. Following this, they "buzzed" the road, flying one after the other, very low and at high speed—contour flying—and one by one disappearing over the hills in front of us. This conduct was frightening these poor refugees who dropped their bundles and hit the dirt. I was incensed by this conduct.

As the last planes passed over, I told Sergeant Fox of two occasions in the States where P-38 pilots had done this sort of thing and paid with their lives when they misjudged and hit the ground, once in Fort Lewis, Washington, and once when Colonel Eisenberg and I stood in our tents in Camp Granite in the Mojave Desert and watched as a pilot buzzed our camp, kicked up the sand with one prop, crashed in our truck park, and burned. I had hardly started relating this incident to Sergeant Fox when the last plane flew over our heads and disappeared out of sight over the hill in front of us. Shortly, there was a loud explosion, a ball of fire, and a black cloud rose to the sky. Another pilot had used this expensive weapon as a toy and had paid for it. I thought, how ironic it was that here I was en route to pay my respects to those thousands who had unwillingly given their lives for this cause, and here was a young man who carelessly threw his life away, and his country gained nothing from it. I wondered that day what his family was told along with that dreaded telegram.

We continued on to the cemetery and returned later to Leipzig with heavy hearts, filled with all sorts of emotions from the experiences of the day.

Now it should be said that this account of events covers the highlights of the experiences by one individual. There were incidents of mortal danger. There were days and nights of mud and snow. There were periods particularly in the Bulge, when I was certain that I would never see home again. Nevertheless, taken as a whole, my experiences were hardly comparable to those of the Infantry, Artillery, and Engineers, as well as others who, month after month, lived and slept in the mud and snow—those who spent days and weeks under enemy fire and still did their jobs. I was in a position where I could almost always see the reason for what we were being asked to do. I was in and out of danger. This was a blessing. It is immeasurably easier to keep your morale up when your battle station is up on the deck rather than down in the boiler room. My hat is off to all my old comrades who slugged it out and made us all proud to be Americans.

Epilogue

The initial contact between American and Soviet troops was made by Major General Emil F. Reinhardt's 69th Infantry Division on April 25th. The contact point was just south of the VII Corps zone and on the following day patrols of the 9th and 104th Divisions met elements of Marshal Koniev's First Ukrainian Army along the Elbe River.

After eleven months of operations under First U.S. Army, VII Corps was placed under operational control of the Ninth U.S. Army on May 6th, as First Army, its European mission accomplished, prepared to become non-operational. On the occasion of the end of the war in Europe (9 May, 1945) and on the separation of VII Corps from Army headquarters, under which it had served during its entire period overseas, Gen. Courtney H. Hodges, the Army commander, addressed the following letter of commendation to Lieutenant General Collins, who had led the Corps through all its combat services:

> On the cessation of hostilities in Germany, I want to congratulate you and to express my appreciation to you, through you to your staff, corps troops, and divisions under your command for the outstanding record you have made since the landing on D-Day, nearly a year ago.
> Your brilliant direction of the rapid advance of VII Corps from Utah Beach to Cherbourg and your successful assault against that vital port contributed significantly toward the establishment of a firm foothold on the continent. Your careful timing and coordination of the successful breakthrough at St. Lô, coupled with the magnificent

fighting qualities of your men resulted in the rapid drive through Northern France and Belgium spearheaded by the VII Corps.

After liberating Liège, with your usual drive and dynamic energy you captured Aachen and advanced to the Roer River. When the Germans attacked on 16 December, your Corps was shifted to the south where it sealed off the point of the enemy penetration, then counter-attacked to hurl the Germans back to the Rhine. Your rapid reduction of Cologne and swift advance across Germany east of the Rhine are a tribute to your outstanding skill as a Commander, and to the selfless devotion to duty you have inspired in your subordinates.

Yours has always been our spearhead corps. I desire to commend you on the outstanding performance of that corps as well as on your own tactical abilities, inspiring leadership, and personal courage.

My best personal wishes to you and to VII Corps for continued success wherever you may go.

Our mission here had been completed. We prepared to leave for the States, knowing that Japan was our next target.

In mid-July the VII Corps headquarters personnel left Leipzig by motor caravan—destination Camp Lucky Strike at Le Havre, France, where we shipped out on the Army troopship *Patrick Henry* for the States. Most of us assumed that upon the completion of our thirty days' rest and recuperation at our homes we would follow our orders and report to Camp San Luis Obispo, California, board our transport ships which were already being loaded, and head for some rendezvous point in the Pacific and then to Japan.

While we were on leave at home, atomic bombs were dropped on Japan on 6 August and 9 August and by 14 August our trip to Japan was not required. They had surrendered.

Many danced in the streets, but for us the release of tension was like letting the air out of a balloon. We had become fatalistic. We'd known our luck had been taxed to its limits and thought these were quite probably our very last days with our families. Now, the ultimate trial we were all geared up to face was not to be. Thank God! Yet so many had not made it this far. Oddly enough, I found it a time for weeping—not for myself, but for those who didn't make it and for the world and its failure to realize what had happened to it.

A Brief Outline of the VII Corps Drive across Europe (1944-45)

6 June	The Utah beachhead established.
6 June to 1 July	Conquest of the Cherbourg Peninsula and capture of the city and port.
1 to 24 July	The slow and bitter battle of the hedgerows.
25 July to 1 Aug	The great breakthrough by way of Marigny.
1 to 6 Aug	Rapid expansion and advance in exploitation of the breakthrough.
7 to 12 Aug	VII Corps troops repel heavy Nazi counterattacks in the defensive battle of Mortain.
13 to 18 Aug	The famous Falaise pocket developed and exploited.
19 Aug to 2 Sept	The Corps pushed rapidly east by a route leading south of Paris. Fourth Infantry Division detached to insure security of Paris.
3 to 5 Sept	In the battle of Mons, 30,000 German troops killed or captured, preventing their occupation of the Siegfried Line.
2 to 12 Sept	Corps troops sweep across Belgium and plunge into Siegfried Line in Germany.

15 Sept	Siegfried Line breached.
16 Sept to 16 Dec	Slow bitter drive to Roer River, including on 21 October of Aachen, first great German city to fall, and Hurtgen Forest fighting.
22 Dec to 25 Jan	End run to stop German advance in Ardennes and eventual reduction of the Belgian Bulge.
25 Jan to 16 March	Corps resume push from Roer River across Cologne Plain. Cologne captured 7 March and Bonn captured 8 March.
16 to 25 March	Expansion of Remagen bridgehead.
25 March to 1 April	All-out attack east into Germany, leading to capture of Altenkirchen, Marsburg, and Paderborn and junction with the 2nd Armored Division at Lippstedt, completing the encirclement of 250,000 enemy troops in the Ruhr pocket.
1 to 26 April	In a resumption of the attack to the east, Corps troops rout the enemy, "pocketing" 85,000 in the Hartz Mountains alone. After capture of Nordhausen, Halle, and Dessau, Corps troops reach their ultimate objective, the Mulde River line.
26 April	Junction with Soviet forces.

The Basics

When small arms fire is coming your way,
And you hear the whine of a ricochet,
You need not bother to duck,
It's already passed; you are in luck!

The one that pops as it goes by the ear,
Is a very near miss; it, you should fear,
A fraction farther to the right—
Sniper would have snuffed your light.

You hear a whine, and a shell explodes,
Just ahead there by the road.
Streamers of smoke from red-hot slivers
Searching the underbrush for your liver.

Your own artillery fire walks ahead;
Stay up close though your feet be lead,
Better one man killed by our own shell burst
Than ten men stitched by machine gun search.

When you walk in a field of red clover,
You are not on a Sunday stroll in Dover,
Watch for wilted clover and loose dirt,
If you step on a mine, you will be hurt!

Castrators, S-Mines, and Mustard Pots
May all be buried in this one plot,
Even a Teller Mine or two
In case a tank comes rolling through.

While I think about it, should I ask?
Have you de-water-proofed your gas mask?
An entrenching spade is a handy tool,
If you left yours behind, you are a fool.

Can you recognize an ME 109 or Spit?
If you can't, you better get on with it,
When a plane comes at you with winking gun,
It's a little late to try and run.

Did you sleep althrough your Basic School?
If you did, that's tough, you were given the tools
To help you survive in a combat zone,
In a body bag, you'll probably go home.

> —Lt. Col. Russell L. Kelch, USA Ret.
> (Reprinted by permission.)